endorsed for
edexcel

Edexcel GCSE (9-1)

History

The American West, c1835–c1895

Series Editor: Angela Leonard   Author: Rob Bircher

ALWAYS LEARNING

PEARSON

Published by Pearson Education Limited, 80 Strand, London, WC2R 0RL.

www.pearsonschoolsandfecolleges.co.uk

Copies of official specifications for all Edexcel qualifications may be found on the website: www.edexcel.com

Text © Pearson Education Limited 2016

Series editor: Angela Leonard
Designed by Colin Tilley Loughrey, Pearson Education Limited
Typeset by Phoenix Photosetting, Chatham, Kent
Original illustrations © Pearson Education Limited
Illustrated by KJA Artists Illustration Agency and Phoenix Photosetting, Chatham, Kent.

Cover design by Colin Tilley Loughrey
Picture research by Christine Martin
Cover photo © Bridgeman Art Library Ltd: Private Collection

The right of Rob Bircher to be identified as author of this work has been asserted by him in accordance with the Copyright, Designs and Patents Act 1988.

First published 2016

2024
10 9 8

British Library Cataloguing in Publication Data
A catalogue record for this book is available from the British Library.
ISBN 978 1 292 12730 9

A note from the publisher
In order to ensure that this resource offers high-quality support for the associated Pearson qualification, it has been through a review process by the awarding body. This process confirms that this resource fully covers the teaching and learning content of the specification or part of a specification at which it is aimed. It also confirms that it demonstrates an appropriate balance between the development of subject skills, knowledge and understanding, in addition to preparation for assessment.

Endorsement does not cover any guidance on assessment activities or processes (e.g. practice questions or advice on how to answer assessment questions), included in the resource nor does it prescribe any particular approach to the teaching or delivery of a related course.

While the publishers have made every attempt to ensure that advice on the qualification and its assessment is accurate, the official specification and associated assessment guidance materials are the only authoritative source of information and should always be referred to for definitive guidance.

Pearson examiners have not contributed to any sections in this resource relevant to examination papers for which they have responsibility.

Examiners will not use endorsed resources as a source of material for any assessment set by Pearson.

Endorsement of a resource does not mean that the resource is required to achieve this Pearson qualification, nor does it mean that it is the only suitable material available to support the qualification, and any resource lists produced by the awarding body shall include this and other appropriate resources.

Websites
Pearson Education Limited is not responsible for the content of any external internet sites. It is essential for tutors to preview each website before using it in class so as to ensure that the URL is still accurate, relevant and appropriate. We suggest that tutors bookmark useful websites and consider enabling students to access them through the school/college intranet.

Contents

How to use this book

What's covered?

This book covers The American West, c1835-c1895. This unit makes up 20% of your GCSE course, and will be examined in Paper 2.

Period studies cover a specific period of time of around 50 years, and require you to know about and be able to analyse the events surrounding important developments and issues that happened in this period. You need to understand how the different topics covered fit into the overall narrative. This book also explains the different types of exam questions you will need to answer, and includes advice and example answers to help you improve.

Features

As well as a clear, detailed explanation of the key knowledge you will need, you will also find a number of features in the book:

Key terms

Where you see a word followed by an asterisk, like this: Frontier*, you will be able to find a Key Terms box on that page that explains what the word means.

> **Key term**
>
> **Frontier***
> The border between two countries, or the border between a 'civilised' country and undeveloped areas.

Activities

Every few pages, you'll find a box containing some activities designed to help check and embed knowledge and get you to really think about what you've studied. The activities start simple, but might get more challenging as you work through them.

Summaries and Checkpoints

At the end of each chunk of learning, the main points are summarised in a series of bullet points – great for embedding the core knowledge, and handy for revision.

Checkpoints help you to check and reflect on your learning. The Strengthen section helps you to consolidate knowledge and understanding, and check that you've grasped the basic ideas and skills. The Challenge questions push you to go beyond just

understanding the information, and into evaluation and analysis of what you've studied.

Sources and Interpretations

Although source work and interpretations do not appear in Paper 2, you'll still find interesting contemporary material throughout the books, showing what people from the period said, thought or created, helping you to build your understanding of people in the past.

The book also includes extracts from the work of historians, showing how experts have interpreted the events you've been studying.

> **Source C**
>
> A photo showing Pinkerton agents. The man sitting down is the son of Alfred Pinkerton, who founded Pinkerton's National Detective Agency in 1850.

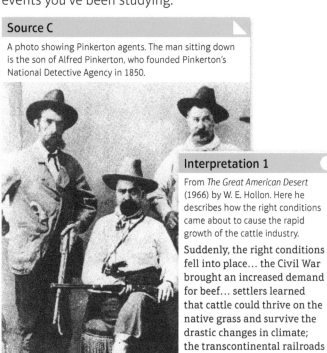

> **Interpretation 1**
>
> From *The Great American Desert* (1966) by W. E. Hollon. Here he describes how the right conditions came about to cause the rapid growth of the cattle industry.
>
> Suddenly, the right conditions fell into place... the Civil War brought an increased demand for beef... settlers learned that cattle could thrive on the native grass and survive the drastic changes in climate; the transcontinental railroads pushed to the Pacific... .

Extend your knowledge

These features contain useful additional information that adds depth to your knowledge, and to your answers. The information is closely related to the key issues in the unit, and questions are sometimes included, helping you to link the new details to the main content.

> **Extend your knowledge**
>
> **Crossing Indian Territory**
>
> The Chisholm Trail went through Indian Territory, the land (now Oklahoma) that had been granted to the eastern tribes of American Indians moved west by the Indian Removal Act (see page 16). These tribes required payment from the cowboys in return for permission to cross their lands. Warriors patrolled the lands to make sure payments were collected. Conflicts sometimes occurred when trail bosses refused to pay.

Exam-style questions and tips

The book also includes extra exam-style questions you can use to practise. These appear in the chapters and are accompanied by a tip to help you get started on an answer.

Exam-style question, Section A

Write a narrative account analysing the ways in which the US government policy towards the Plains Indians developed in the period 1835–51.

You may use the following in your answer:

- the Permanent Indian Frontier (c1834)
- the Indian Appropriations Act (1851)

You **must** also use information of your own. **8 marks**

Exam tip

Plan your answer first by listing the main developments of 1835–51 in sequence. This will help you structure your answer and think about how one event links to the next.

Recap pages

At the end of each chapter, you'll find a page designed to help you to consolidate and reflect on the chapter as a whole. Each recap page includes a recall quiz, ideal for quickly checking your knowledge or for revision. Recap pages also include activities designed to help you summarise and analyse what you've learned, and also reflect on how each chapter links to other parts of the unit.

 THINKING HISTORICALLY

These activities are designed to help you develop a better understanding of how history is constructed, and are focused on the key areas of Evidence, Interpretations, Cause & Consequence and Change & Continuity. In the Period Study, you will come across an activity on Cause & Consequence, as this is a key focus for this unit.

The Thinking Historically approach has been developed in conjunction with Dr Arthur Chapman and the Institute of Education, UCL. It is based on research into the misconceptions that can hold students back in history.

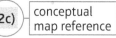 **THINKING HISTORICALLY** Cause and Consequence (2c) — conceptual map reference

The Thinking Historically conceptual map can be found at: www.pearsonschools.co.uk/thinkinghistoricallygcse

 **WRITING HISTORICALLY**

At the end of most chapters is a spread dedicated to helping you improve your writing skills. These include simple techniques you can use in your writing to make your answers clearer, more precise and better focused on the question you're answering.

The Writing Historically approach is based on the *Grammar for Writing* pedagogy developed by a team at the University of Exeter and popular in many English departments. Each spread uses examples from the preceding chapter, so it's relevant to what you've just been studying.

Preparing for your exams

At the back of the book, you'll find a special section dedicated to explaining and exemplifying the new Edexcel GCSE History exams. Advice on the demands of this paper, written by Angela Leonard, helps you prepare for and approach the exam with confidence. Each question type is explained through annotated sample answers at two levels, showing clearly how answers can be improved.

Pearson Progression Scale: This icon indicates the Step that a sample answer has been graded at on the Pearson Progression Scale.

This book is also available as an online ActiveBook, which can be licensed for your whole institution.

There is also an ActiveLearn Digital Service available to support delivery of this book, featuring a front-of-class version of the book, lesson plans, worksheets, exam practice PowerPoints, assessments, notes on Thinking Historically and Writing Historically, and more.

ActiveLearn
Digital Service

Timeline: The American West, c1835–c1895

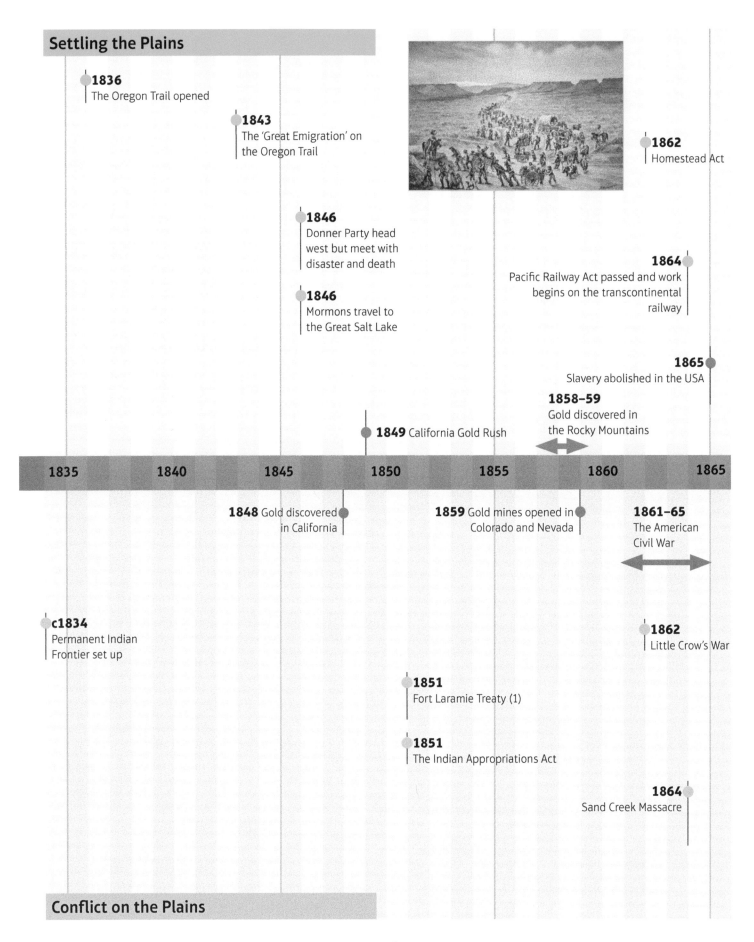

Settling the Plains

1836
The Oregon Trail opened

1843
The 'Great Emigration' on the Oregon Trail

1846
Donner Party head west but meet with disaster and death

1846
Mormons travel to the Great Salt Lake

1862
Homestead Act

1864
Pacific Railway Act passed and work begins on the transcontinental railway

1865
Slavery abolished in the USA

1858–59
Gold discovered in the Rocky Mountains

1849 California Gold Rush

| 1835 | 1840 | 1845 | 1850 | 1855 | 1860 | 1865 |

1848 Gold discovered in California

1859 Gold mines opened in Colorado and Nevada

1861–65
The American Civil War

c1834
Permanent Indian Frontier set up

1862
Little Crow's War

1851
Fort Laramie Treaty (1)

1851
The Indian Appropriations Act

1864
Sand Creek Massacre

Conflict on the Plains

1866
Goodnight and Loving reach Fort Sumner with a herd of cattle

1867
Abilene becomes the first cow town

1869
First Transcontinental Railroad completed

1870
Cattle Ranching begins on the Plains, leading to the 'Open Range'

1873
Timber Culture Act

1874
Barbed wire begins to be mass-produced

1874
Wind-powered water pump introduced

1879
Exoduster Movement

1881
The OK Corral

1886–87
Severe winter leads to the end of the open range

1892
Johnson County War

1893
Oklahoma Land Rush

| 1870 | 1875 | 1880 | 1885 | 1890 | 1895 |

1866
Fetterman's Trap

1866–68
Red Cloud's War

1874
Custer leads expedition to the Black Hills

1885
All Plains Indians are resettled on to reservations

1868
'The Winter Campaign'

1876–81
The Great Sioux War

1887
Dawes Act

1868
President Grant's 'Peace Policy'

1868
Fort Laramie Treaty (2)

1876
The Battle of the Little Big Horn

1890
Wounded Knee Massacre

1890
The US government closes Frontier

01 | The early settlement of the West, c1835–c1862

The American West is the two-thirds of the USA that is west of the Mississippi River, a vast expanse of land with many different landscapes. The area is dominated by the Great Plains, a huge natural grassland that once stretched from north to south through the middle of the USA. In the early 19th century, the white Americans, who had colonised the eastern third of the USA, called the Plains 'The Great American Desert'. They were happy to leave it to the American Indians (sometimes called Native Americans) who were the native people of the land. The American Indians who lived in the Plains were called Plains Indians by white Americans and they had developed sophisticated ways of survival on the Plains, dependent on two animals: the buffalo and the horse.

By 1840, the US government had forced all Plains Indians to live to the west of a Permanent Indian Frontier, running along the edge of the Great Plains. The government believed it was not possible for American Indians and whites to live together until American Indians had learned how to live in a 'civilised' way, like white people. But through the 1840s, new developments brought changes to both the East and West that 'pushed' and 'pulled' people to move west to Oregon and California and encouraged them to make a living farming the Plains. The growing number of settlers moving across the Plains led to tensions between settlers and Plains Indians. In 1851, the US government granted land and protection to the Plains Indians in return for promises not to attack the settlers. But tensions only grew stronger.

Mass migration to the West, following the California Gold Rush, also caused major problems because of a lack of law enforcement. As a result, mining communities took on law enforcement for themselves, but this did not solve the problem.

Learning outcomes

By the end of this chapter, you will:

- understand the way of life and beliefs of the Plains Indians
- understand why white Americans migrated westwards and why this migration was challenging
- understand why conflict and tension developed between different groups of people in the West.

1.1 The Plains Indians: their beliefs and way of life

Learning outcomes

- Understand the ways of life of the Plains Indians.
- Understand the Plains Indians' beliefs about land and nature, and their attitudes to war and property.
- Understand the US government support for westward expansion and the significance of the Permanent Indian Frontier (c1834) and the Indian Appropriations Act (1851).

Who were the Plains Indians?

Many different American Indian tribes made up the people known as the Plains Indians. Figure 1.1 shows some of the main Plains Indian tribes and roughly where they lived on the Great Plains. Some tribes, such as the **Sioux**, were so large that they were called nations. Several tribes were sworn enemies and would fight on sight – one example of this was the Sioux and the Pawnee. Others were traditional allies. Some made and broke alliances as conditions changed and, in particular, as white Americans began to venture on to the Great Plains.

Plains Indian society

Many different tribes lived on the Great Plains. Each tribe was made up of different bands. Bands could be several hundred people or just 20 or 30 people.

In order to survive, it was essential that the different bands within a tribe worked together. All the different bands in a tribe would usually meet in the summer for a great tribal camp. As well as being social and religious occasions, these were times when a tribe could co-operate to ensure their survival on the Plains.

Different tribes had different ways of organising their bands. For some tribes, like the Comanches, bands came together frequently and people often moved between bands. For others, like the Pawnee, each band had a separate village.

The Sioux nation was one of the biggest nations. It was made up of the Lakota, Dakota and Nakota tribes. The Lakota was made up of seven sub-tribes, including the Oglala and Hunkpapa.

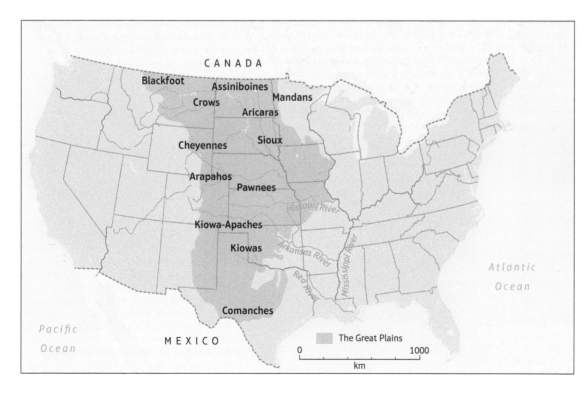

Figure 1.1 Locations of the main Plains Indian tribes.

9

Chiefs and councils

Chiefs were the leaders of Plains Indian society. They were always men. Each tribe could have many chiefs: a war chief, a spiritual chief and a chief who led negotiations with other tribes. White Americans (of the time) found this difficult to understand and this led to problems in the relationships between the US government and the Plains Indians.

- There was no single system for choosing chiefs. Chiefs were valued because of their wisdom, leadership and spiritual powers or for their skill as warriors or hunters. Chiefs were rarely chiefs for life. They came and went as their skills emerged and, in time, faded away.
- Each band had a band chief, who was chosen to guide the band in finding enough to eat and protecting the band from danger.
- Band chiefs and elders made up the tribe's council when the tribe came together. In some tribes, the council could declare war on another tribe, or negotiate a peace treaty with another tribe.
- Everyone could give their opinion in the council and was listened to. The tribe's spiritual chief would be consulted on important decisions. No decision was made until everyone at the council had agreed to it.
- In tribes like the Lakota Sioux, chiefs had no power to command their people. Bands made their own decisions. Some bands might follow one chief and others would choose a different leader.

Famous chiefs

Some chiefs became famous because of their leadership in wars against the white Americans. However, not all people in their tribes agreed with them, or followed them. For example, **Red Cloud** (see Figure 1.2) was a Lakota Sioux chief who brought together Sioux and Cheyenne tribes in 'Red Cloud's War' against white Americans (see page 66). The war forced the US government to pull the army out of Sioux lands, in return for peace. However, not all the Sioux agreed with Red Cloud's peace treaty with the US government. Many Sioux followed a chief called **Sitting Bull** (see Figure 1.3), who rejected the peace treaty, and a chief called **Crazy Horse** (see Figure 1.4). Sitting Bull had a vision of white soldiers 'as thick as grasshoppers' falling down into the Lakota Sioux camp, which inspired many Sioux to fight the US Army.

Figure 1.2 Red Cloud was a chief of the Oglala sub-tribe of the Lakota people of the Sioux nation. He was born c1822 and became a very important Lakota war leader.

Figure 1.3 Sitting Bull was a chief of the Hunkpapa sub-tribe of the Lakota Sioux. He was born c1831. An experienced warrior, Sitting Bull was also a famous holy man.

Figure 1.4 Crazy Horse was a war leader of the Oglala Sioux. He was born c1842 and was a respected warrior. He was also famous for his ability to enter the spirit world through visions.

Warrior brotherhoods

As well as bands and the tribal council, Plains Indians also had warrior **brotherhoods**. There were several different brotherhoods within a tribe and young men joined after proving their bravery and skill in fighting with other tribes. Within the Lakota Sioux, some of the brotherhoods included the White Horse Riders, the Strong Hearts and the Crow Owners.

- Warrior brotherhoods were important for all Plains Indian tribes because they trained young men in fighting skills. They also taught young men about the tribe's beliefs and values.
- Warrior brotherhoods, like bands, were not under the command of the tribal council in many Plains Indian tribes. This meant that they might not always respect any peace treaties.
- Leading men from the brotherhoods were also invited to join a guard unit for the whole tribe, which also organised the tribe's yearly buffalo hunt, made sure old and ill tribe members were fed, and chose where the tribe should gather to make camp.

Activity ?

The US government officials were often frustrated that when they agreed a treaty with the chief of the tribe, many of the Plains Indians then failed to follow the agreements set out in the treaty. Use the information about chiefs on pages 10 and 11 to write a short explanation for this behaviour.

Extend your knowledge

The Last Child society

Crazy Horse, the warrior chief from the Oglala Sioux, started a warrior brotherhood called 'the Last Child society', which was made up only of youngest sons. Crazy Horse's thinking was that the youngest son always tries to impress his brothers and sisters and so the 'last child' would be the bravest and most daring.

Women and Plains Indian society

Women could not be chiefs and a successful man could have more than one wife in Plains Indian society. Women were responsible for feeding and clothing their families; and for their family's possessions. Women were also responsible for processing buffalo hides and meat, turning them into products that could be traded.

This sounds as if women were not valued in Plains Indian society. In fact, the reverse was true, their roles were respected very highly. Both men and women had set roles that could not change. This was because everyone needed to perform their specialised role with great skill if the tribe was to survive.

Survival on the Great Plains

The Great Plains have very hot summers and extremely cold winters. The Plains are also very dry, with very little surface water (streams or rivers). When rain comes, it is often in thunderstorms. Lightning flashes sometimes ignited raging fires that swept across the Plains, burning the dry grass and anything else caught in their way. These fires could be whipped up by the strong winds that also blow across the Plains.

Survival on the Plains depended on hunting buffalo on horseback. Huge herds of buffalo migrated across the Plains in search of fresh grass. The Plains Indians followed the buffalo migrations through the summer and autumn. As a consequence, Plains Indians had developed:

- amazing horse-riding and archery skills, so they could ride amongst stampeding buffalo, shooting arrows into their sides to kill them
- a travelling (nomadic) lifestyle: tipis* to live in (these could be taken down and packed for travel in ten minutes) and travois* to carry each family's belongings over the Plains to their next camp
- skills to use every part of the buffalo (and other animals) for food, fuel (buffalo dung), clothing, shelter, ornaments, gifts and toys. Buffalo meat was preserved by drying it in the Sun
- a reverence (deep respect) for buffalo and the other animals they depended on. Plains Indians believed that all nature and the land itself must be treated with great respect or the spirits that lived in everything would no longer agree to help the Plains Indians survive.

In the harsh winters of the Great Plains, most tribes moved into lodges: these were circular buildings made of earth and timber logs. First, a framework of strong logs was made, and then earth was piled on top to create a well-insulated living space. A fire pit was made in the middle with beds on platforms around the walls. Some lodges were big enough for 60 people to live in. They were built in sheltered valleys, clustered together to help protect the bands from attack.

Key terms

Tipis*

Tent-like homes of Plains Indian families, made of animal hide stretched over wooden poles. The strong, flexible pyramid shape of the tipi meant it could stand up to strong winds.

Travois*

A framework harnessed to a horse or dog on which Plains Indians transported their belongings.

Source A

A painting by Charles Marion Russell showing Plains Indians pursuing a herd of buffalo across the Great Plains. It was painted in 1887.

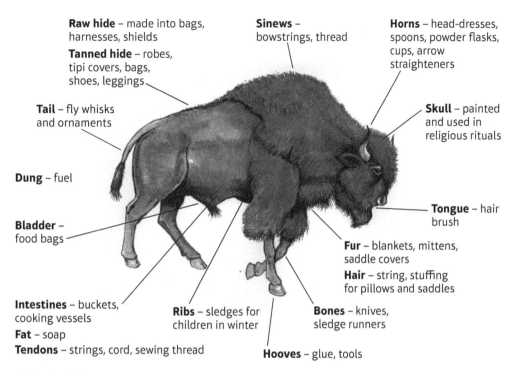

Raw hide – made into bags, harnesses, shields

Tanned hide – robes, tipi covers, bags, shoes, leggings

Sinews – bowstrings, thread

Horns – head-dresses, spoons, powder flasks, cups, arrow straighteners

Tail – fly whisks and ornaments

Skull – painted and used in religious rituals

Dung – fuel

Tongue – hair brush

Bladder – food bags

Fur – blankets, mittens, saddle covers

Hair – string, stuffing for pillows and saddles

Intestines – buckets, cooking vessels

Fat – soap

Tendons – strings, cord, sewing thread

Ribs – sledges for children in winter

Bones – knives, sledge runners

Hooves – glue, tools

Figure 1.5 The uses of the buffalo.

The importance of horses to Plains Indians

Horses were essential to Plains Indians: they needed them to hunt buffalo and to travel across the Plains in the search for food. Horses were also highly significant for warfare and for status within Plains Indian society. Men measured their wealth in horses. Raids on other tribes or white settlers* were often to steal horses. In the 1870s, the 2,900 Hunkpapa Sioux sub-tribe had 3,500 horses while, in the south of the Plains, the Comanche had nearly 8,000 horses in a tribe of 3,000 people.

Key term

White settlers*

European migrants to America (and their descendants) who made up a large proportion of the US citizens settling in the West.

Beliefs about nature and land

Beliefs about nature

Plains Indians believed that everything in nature had a spirit. These spirits would sometimes help humans. The Plains Indians believed that humans were a part of nature and should work with the spirits of nature rather than trying to tame nature to obey them.

Activities

1   Describe two solutions which the Plains Indians had developed to cope with the tough climate conditions of the Great Plains.

2   Chiefs were chosen for their skills in particular areas. Work in groups to choose three chiefs with three different skills, such as: a chief who remembers what the homework was, a humour chief or a chief who gives sensible advice. Make a list of the advantages and disadvantages of being one of three chiefs you have chosen.

3   The US government wanted the Plains Indians to stop moving around and stay in one area. What would three consequences of this have been for the way of life of the Plains Indians?

Plains Indians believed they could contact the spirit world through 'vision quests', guided by spirit animals, like spirit hawks or spirit foxes. Plains Indians also danced special ritual dances, like the Sun Dance, to enter the spirit world. It was also possible to work with spirits to charge up magic items, which Plains Indians would wear to bring them luck in hunting or protection from weapons, including bullets.

Beliefs about land and property

Land was seen as sacred – the 'mother' of the Plains Indians. Some lands were especially sacred. For the Lakota Sioux, the Paha Sapa, the Black Hills of South Dakota, were the most sacred of all. The Lakota believed their people had been created in a special cave in these hills by the Great Spirit.

Some Plains Indian tribes farmed land as well as living by hunting, fishing and gathering wild plant resources. In these cases, a farming plot did belong to a family rather than the whole tribe using all the land together. However, over most of the Plains, the land was very difficult to farm and no one person or family owned this land as their property. This land was not something that could be bought or sold. All Plains Indian tribes did have hunting areas that they used together. Sometimes treaties were agreed between tribes to share these hunting areas. When food resources were scarce, conflicts occurred as tribes pushed into hunting areas that were traditionally used by others.

Farming or mining were seen by some Plains Indians as disrespectful to the land. These activities in sacred places would be especially likely to disrupt the sacred link between the tribe and the spirits.

Attitudes to war

Survival on the Plains was so difficult that it is not surprising that Plains Indian tribes raided each other for food, horses, weapons and people (women to marry and children to bring up in their tribe). However, because young men were very valuable to the tribe as hunters and protectors, no tribe could afford to lose many warriors in fights. As a result, Plains Indians developed several ways to minimise the number of young men who were killed or maimed in raids.

- The raid would only go ahead if it looked as if it would work, and the raiders would escape as quickly as they could if there was too much opposition. This was very unlike white American soldiers, who had been trained to believe that a soldier should never run away.
- Only selected brotherhoods would go on a raid. This reduced the tribe's losses if the raid failed.

- 'Counting coup': coup means success. Counting coup was special type of fighting in which a warrior would attempt to hit or touch (rather than kill) an enemy and get away again without being injured or killed. It demanded huge levels of skill and bravery, and success gained the warrior a lot of respect and honour from the rest of the tribe.

Interpretation 1

From *The Cheyennes* (1978) by E. A. Hoebel.

War was transformed into a great game in which scoring against the enemy often took precedence [more importance] over killing him. The scoring was in the counting coup – touching or striking an enemy with hand or weapons. Coups counted within an enemy encampment ranked the highest of all. A man's rank as a warrior depended on two factors: his total 'score' in coups, and his ability to lead successful raids in which Cheyenne losses were low.

Activity

Plains Indians' beliefs about land and nature and their attitude to war and fighting had important consequences for relations between Plains Indian tribes and white settlers. Using what you know, explain what you think Plains Indian attitudes towards the following situations would have been.

- a White settlers fence off land that the tribe uses for hunting and then plough it for crops.
- b White people start mining for gold in the Black Hills area of South Dakota.
- c The US government tells the chiefs of the tribal council that the warrior brotherhoods must stay away from white people travelling through the tribe's hunting lands.
- d The US government insists that Plains Indian teenagers should go to school in white cities and learn about Christianity.

The US government policy towards the Plains Indians

All through the 19th century, the US federal* government struggled for a solution to 'the Indian problem' as the number of white Americans in the West grew and conflict between whites and Plains Indians over land increased. The US government had two main approaches to tackling this conflict:

- keeping white settlers and Plains Indians apart
- encouraging Plains Indians to become like white settlers.

It was very hard to follow both approaches at the same time, since keeping Plains Indians away from white Americans meant that they continued to follow their traditional ways of life rather than learning white ways.

Timeline

Key events in Plains Indian policy, 1830–1851

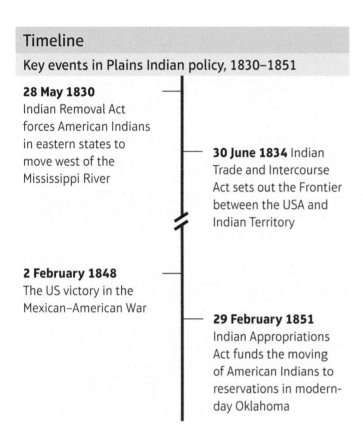

28 May 1830
Indian Removal Act forces American Indians in eastern states to move west of the Mississippi River

30 June 1834 Indian Trade and Intercourse Act sets out the Frontier between the USA and Indian Territory

2 February 1848
The US victory in the Mexican–American War

29 February 1851
Indian Appropriations Act funds the moving of American Indians to reservations in modern-day Oklahoma

> ### Key term
>
> **Federal***
>
> The USA is a union of states. Each state has its own state government and then there is a federal government: a government over all the states.

> ### Extend your knowledge
>
> **American Indians and the federal government**
>
> Individual US states were not allowed to negotiate with American Indians (including the Plains Indians): they were the responsibility of the federal government and not of the state or states that they lived in. This provided American Indians with some protection because state governments were often openly hostile towards American Indian populations and very keen to get hold of their land. But the relationship between American Indians and the federal government was entirely unequal. Federal government viewed the American Indians as being like children who needed to be kept safe while they were guided towards a civilised way of life. American Indians' rights as the original inhabitants of the land were not given any respect and their deep understanding of their environment and how to manage its resources was largely ignored.

Conflicts over land

White Americans recognised that the Plains Indians had some rights to American land because they had lived on their lands for a long time. However, most white Americans also thought that Plains Indians were savages who did nothing to improve the land: they just lived off the resources the land produced naturally. That meant, they thought, that white Americans had better rights to own land because they were trying to improve it: ploughing it for farming, digging up its minerals for manufacturing, clearing its forests for timber and developing America into a civilised country.

As a result, it seemed wrong to most white Americans that Plains Indians should have good land; land that white Americans could really benefit from. They felt that either the Plains Indians should learn to farm the land and make it productive, or they should move off it and let others farm it instead.

A 'permanent' Indian Frontier*

In 1830, President Jackson signed the **Indian Removal Act**, which pressured 46,000 American Indians living in the east of America into moving to new lands west of the Mississippi River. Jackson promised that they would never have to give up this new land, known as **Indian Territory**, and that they would be protected from Plains Indian tribes who already lived there and from white settlers.

> ### Key term
> **Frontier***
> The border between two countries, or the border between a 'civilised' country and undeveloped areas.

Then, in 1834, the US government passed the Indian Trade and Intercourse Act that said that Indian Territory was: 'all that part of the United States west of the Mississippi [River] and not within the states of Missouri and Louisiana, or the territory of Arkansas'. To keep Plains Indians and whites apart, the government established a '**permanent**' Indian Frontier (see Figure 1.6).

The 1834 Act also prohibited whites from settling on American Indian lands, prevented the sale of any guns or alcohol to American Indians by white traders and gave the US Army the role of policing the Frontier. The Frontier was guarded by a chain of US Army forts connected by a military road.

Westward expansion

In the 1830s, a few white Americans thought that the land behind the Indian Frontier was worth having. The Great Plains were not suitable for farming using the methods then available (it was known as 'The Great American Desert' because of its tough climate). Although the US Army could not hope to control the whole of the vast Frontier, there were not enough whites wanting to cross the Frontier to cause major problems in the 1830s.

However, in the late 1840s, the situation changed. The USA won a war with Mexico in 1848 and, as a result, the USA gained huge new territories in the West, including California. In 1846, the USA had also gained control over its territory in Oregon Country (which had previously been shared with Britain) and, in 1845, Texas officially became part of the USA. This expansion of the USA had major consequences for American Indian policy. Instead of the Indian Frontier dividing the American Indians in the West from the white Americans in the East, American Indian lands were now in the middle of the USA.

Government support for westward expansion

The US government wanted US citizens to move into its new territories in the West. Although settlers could travel by sea to the west coast, it was a very long and expensive journey. People needed to be able to travel safely across Plains Indian lands.

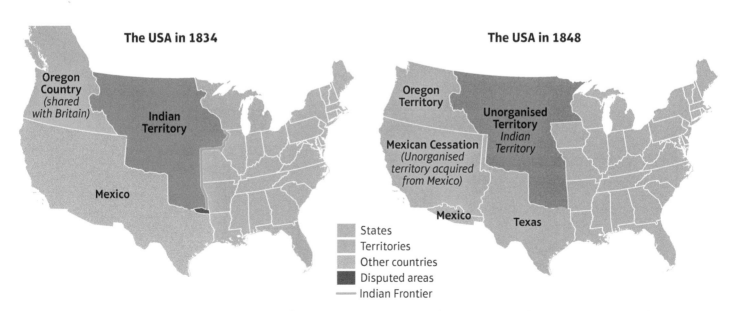

Figure 1.6 Changes in the development of the USA from 1834 to 1848. It shows the USA in 1834 when the Permanent Indian Frontier was established and the USA in 1848, when Texas had joined the USA as a state, and new territories were added in the West.

People travelling to the West followed trails*. The US government used its army to force Plains Indians to move away from the trails and stop them attacking the travellers. This meant that US policy started to change. The Permanent Indian Frontier still marked the boundary with Plains Indian lands, but it was no longer the case that whites could not cross the Frontier.

The Indian Appropriations Act (1851)

In 1851, the US government passed the Indian Appropriations Act. This provided government money to pay for moving Plains Indians in Indian Territory onto reservations*. Hunting lands were also allocated to some reservations, so the Plains Indians could continue to hunt buffalo and other animals.

Reservations were a continuation of the government policy of moving American Indians away from land that white people wanted to use, but they were something new, too. By reducing the amount of land Plains Indians had available for hunting, the government hoped to encourage them to take up farming. The idea was that once Plains Indians became farmers, they could begin to live like white Americans.

Key terms

Trails*

Routes marking out 'tried-and-tested' ways across the West.

Reservation*

An area of land 'reserved' for use by American Indians and managed by the federal government.

Exam-style question, Section A

Write a narrative account analysing the ways in which the US government policy towards the Plains Indians developed in the period 1835–51.

You may use the following in your answer:

- the Permanent Indian Frontier (c1834)
- the Indian Appropriations Act (1851)

You **must** also use information of your own. **8 marks**

Exam tip

Plan your answer first by listing the main developments of 1835–51 in sequence. This will help you structure your answer and think about how one event links to the next.

Summary

- The Plains Indians were made up of many different tribes and nations, with some very different customs.
- The Plains Indians' ideas about land, nature, warfare and property were very different from those of the white Americans who were starting to settle on the Plains.
- The US government supported the westward expansion of the USA. At first, tribes from the East were moved behind a Permanent Indian Frontier, then moved to live within reservations to keep them and whites apart.

Checkpoint

Strengthen

S1 Which of these came first: the Indian Appropriations Act, the end of the war with Mexico or the creation of a Permanent Indian Frontier?

Challenge

C1 Explain the importance of the buffalo to the Plains Indians.

C2 Explain the importance of the horse to the Plains Indians.

How confident do you feel about your answers to these questions? If you are not sure, it might help to start a timeline for the whole period covered by this chapter: from the 1830s to 1862.

1.2 Migration and early settlement

What factors encouraged migration west?

There were many different factors involved in people's decisions to make the long and dangerous trek west. Some factors 'pushed' migrants away from the East, while others 'pulled' them to the West.

Economic conditions in the East

In 1837, there was an economic crisis in the East and South of the USA, which lasted until the mid-1840s. Many banks collapsed, people lost their savings, businesses failed and thousands lost their jobs. In some areas, unemployment was as high as 25%. Those who still had a job faced wage cuts of as much as 40%. These problems were 'push' factors. They gave people good reasons to try to make a new life in another part of the USA.

Farmland in Oregon

Traders and fur-trappers had been travelling to Oregon (on the USA's Pacific coast) for many years, and they passed back news of the rich farming land west of the Rocky Mountains. The promise of free farming land in the West was a powerful 'pull' factor, especially as economic conditions worsened in the East.

However, the sea-route to Oregon was expensive – it cost at least $300 at a time when a farm labourer could expect to earn $11 a month. It also took as long as a year to make the trip round South America and up the west coast of the USA. Migrants needed an overland route that wagons could travel on so they could transport everything they needed to set up a new life in the West. However, although the Plains were flat and comparatively easy to travel over, the high mountain ranges of the Rockies and Sierra Nevada formed an enormous barrier. A way through the mountains for wagons was needed before overland migration to Oregon could begin.

The Oregon Trail

The Oregon Trail was the only practical way for migrants to get across the mountains with wagons. This made it vitally important to the settlement of the West and a powerful 'pull' factor, encouraging migration west too. The key part of the route, the South Pass in the Rocky Mountains, was first publicised by an explorer called Jedidiah Smith in 1825. Fur-trappers started to use the route, digging out a path through gullies, clearing scrub vegetation and finding the best spots to cross rivers.

The numbers of migrants using the Oregon Trail grew and grew as people were 'pushed' from the east by economic problems and 'pulled' west by the opportunity of a new start. By 1869, when the Oregon Trail was replaced as the main way of travelling west by the First Transcontinental Railroad, 400,000 people had migrated along the Oregon Trail.

The first migrants to travel the Oregon Trail with a covered wagon reached their destination in 1836. They were two married couples, Narcissa and Marcus Whitman and Henry and Eliza Spalding. They were all missionaries* who travelled to Oregon to convert American Indian tribes there to Christianity. Their success established the Oregon Trail as a route for migrants. In 1840, the Walker family (including five children) completed the Trail. In 1841, a party of 60 people made the trip, 100 people in 1842, and, in 1843, 900 people. This proved that large numbers of people could make the journey. The 1843 trip was called the 'Great Emigration' and was led by Marcus Whitman.

Key term

Missionaries*
Someone who travels to a place in order to convert its people to their faith.

Figure 1.7
The Oregon Trail 1836.

Government help

The US government encouraged people to move to Oregon because they wanted to establish it as US territory instead of sharing it with the British. In 1841, the US government provided $30,000 for an expedition to map the Oregon Trail and publish reports that would help migrants to get to Oregon. John Fremont led the expedition and his reports made travelling the Trail sound exciting and achievable. The reports became the guidebook that migrants used on the Trail: another important 'pull' factor to convince people that the risks of moving to Oregon were manageable. By 1846, more than 5,000 people had migrated west along the Oregon Trail.

The Gold Rush of 1849

In April 1849, 100,000 people left the East to travel to California. This huge increase was because gold had been discovered in the Sierra Nevada in California the year before. Thousands travelled along the Oregon Trail, thousands more travelled from all over the world, by land and sea, in the hope of finding gold: gold was the ultimate 'pull' factor that meant California's population reached 300,000 by 1855. Although a few did became very rich, most men were unsuccessful and either went back home or settled in California. Many of those that stayed became farmers.

California's population boomed and its economy grew rapidly. The prospectors* needed equipment, food, drink, and entertainment, which attracted more people to the West to become shopkeepers, bartenders and traders. This was exactly what the US government had hoped for in the West. There were now plenty of US citizens living in California, which made it much less likely that another country would try to take it from the USA. Also, California's gold, and its successful economy, was helping the USA to recover from the economic crisis.

Key term

Prospector*
Someone who searches for gold or other precious metals, looking for signs of the metals in rocky outcrops or in the silt of streams and river beds.

The **Gold Rush** had other consequences for the development of the West.

- It promoted the image of the West as the place where individuals could make a success of their lives, get a new start, and be free and independent.
- Farming in California grew. California's excellent farmland meant that it was soon exporting food products all over the world.
- Money from the Gold Rush helped pay for the First Transcontinental Railroad in 1869 (see page 42).

Not all consequences were positive, however:

- the rapid growth of mining towns led to problems of law and order (see page 31)
- the new migrants murdered or enslaved California Indians to get them out of their way.

19

Source A

In 1860, the US government asked the artist Emanuel Leutze to paint a picture that put the concept of 'Manifest Destiny' into visual form. The picture's title is *Westward the course of Empire takes its way*.

Manifest Destiny

Another 'pull' factor in migration to the West was the belief that white Americans had the right to populate all areas of America from coast to coast. White Americans, such as John Fremont (see page 19), were inspired by this idea for many years. The government was keen to encourage this belief, which was expressed in the phrase '**Manifest Destiny**'*.

Key term

Manifest Destiny*

The belief that it was God's will for white people to take possession of the whole of the USA and make it productive and civilised.

The significance of 'Manifest Destiny' was that it carried the sense of an inevitable process: like a scientific law or God's will. As a result, white Americans might feel sorry for American Indians who had to be cleared out of the way of white settlers, but it was 'Manifest Destiny': the white race had been given a mission by God to civilise America, to make it productive and to populate it from coast to coast.

Activities

1   The following events, dates and consequences have been muddled up. Sort them so each event is with its correct date and a consequence that follows on from it.

Event	Date	Consequence
Gold is discovered in the Sierra Nevada.	1836	This starts the use of the Oregon Trail by migrants.
Financial crisis in the USA.	1837	Positive reports about how easy the Oregon Trail was to travel convinced large groups of people to migrate west
Fremont commissioned to survey the Oregon Trail.	1841	100,000 people travel to California in 1849 by land.
The first migrants reach Oregon.	1848	Unemployment and low wages meant many people were desperate for a new start in the West.

2   After reading through all the factors that encouraged people to migrate west, which one do you think was the most important, and why?

3   Why do you think the artist of Source A chose this scene to express the idea of 'Manifest Destiny' in a painting? With a partner, describe the message that the painting expresses.

The process and problems of migration

The Oregon Trail was 3,200 km long, starting from the Missouri river and ending in the Willamette Valley, Oregon. Migrants splitting off the Oregon Trail and heading to California had a 3,800 km trip in total. The journey was a major challenge and migrants needed to plan each stage carefully.

- Migrants needed to complete their journey before winter because otherwise they were likely to get stuck in the mountains and freeze to death.

- Migrants were advised not to begin the journey until April. This gave enough time for fresh grass to grow on the Plains after winter and provide food for their animals.

- Migrants needed to take enough food to live on for the whole journey, as well as essentials for setting up their new home. Most people lived on salt pork, because it did not rot for a long time.

- The best animals to pull the fully-loaded wagons were oxen: very strong, obedient and able to live on the grass and sage bushes of the Plains. However, oxen were very slow: they moved at 3 km an hour. This slow progress meant time was very tight. With an April start, there could be no delays if the migrants were to get through the mountains before winter.

- Most wagon 'trains' (the name given to the long line of wagons) ended up with at least 20 wagons and some had many more. It was safest to travel in large groups with people that had a range of skills: for example, a carpenter to help repair damage to the wagons, hunters and fishermen to provide food, and people with medical skills.

Problems

The main problems were getting stuck, falling ill, or running out of supplies. At least 20,000 people are thought to have died along the Trail, many from drowning and some from accidents (such as being crushed under a wagon's wheels).

The biggest killer was cholera. Cholera was a consequence of everyone following the same tried-and-tested migration process. Each wagon train used the same spots for campsites and popular spots were by rivers. Migrants used rivers for drinking water, but also to go to the toilet in. This spread disease, especially cholera.

Many migrants dreaded attacks by Plains Indians, but, in fact, most settlers' diaries record no mention of conflict. Plains Indians were more likely to help migrants through the mountains than attack them. However, white settlers' fears led to calls for government protection for migrants (see page 27 for more on this).

The experiences of the Donner Party

The Donner Party was a group of 300 migrants, in 60 wagons. The group, led by the Donner brothers, started the Oregon Trail in May 1846. They were well equipped, although the group had more elderly people, women and children than was usual.

By July, when they had reached Fort Bridger in the Rocky Mountains, the group split. Around 80 migrants, including both Donner brothers, decided to try a new short cut that left the Oregon Trail and cut some 550 km off the established route. A trail guide, called Lansford Hastings, had written about this short cut in a guidebook. It was described as a fine road with plenty of grass and water. What the migrants did not know was that Hastings had not used the short cut himself – he simply **thought** it should work.

The short cut turned out to be anything but short. Instead of saving time, this route caused delay after delay. Unlike the well-established Oregon Trail, where migrants could just follow the ruts left by the wagon wheels of previous travellers, this route had not been marked out and was hard to follow. While the Oregon Trail had been cleared for wagons, here the terrain was rugged and rocky, with steep slopes and deep canyons. The party had to try out different spots to cross rivers before they found the safest point to cross – unlike the Oregon Trail where river ferries waited to transfer migrants across (for a fee). There were also stretches of desert with no water or grass for the livestock, with none of the Oregon Trail's forts where migrants could take on new provisions and places where livestock could find pasture. Arguments raged constantly within the group as to what they should do – keep going or turn back. It was mid-October when the Donner Party reached the Sierra Nevada Mountains.

At the start of November, the exhausted oxen had dragged the wagons high into the mountains, but before they could make it over the pass, snow storms trapped the Donner Party. Their livestock died and soon their food ran out. The first migrant died of starvation on 15 December. When rescuers from California reached the party in February, only half of the original 80 were alive – and most of those had only survived by eating those that had died.

Source B

Captain Fellun, who led one of the rescue parties, described what he found when he reached the Donner party in February 1847.

```
A horrible scene presented itself. Human
bodies terribly mutilated, legs, arms and
skulls scattered in every direction. At the
mouth of a tent stood a large pot, filled with
human flesh cut up. It was the body of George
Donner. His head had been split open and the
brains extracted.
```

The Mormon migration, 1846–47

The experiences of the Donner Party showed what could go wrong when migrants did not follow an established trail and the necessary processes for survival. The experiences of the **Mormons** were different, even though they too struck out for a new destination away from the Oregon Trail.

The Mormons were a religious group that was shunned by other Christians because of some of their practices, such as polygamy (where a man could marry several wives at once). The Mormons were forced to move from one state to another, with opposition to them growing everywhere they went.

In 1845, the Mormons were ordered to leave Illinois after rioters murdered their leader, Joseph Smith. Their new leader, Brigham Young, believed God had called on the Mormons to migrate to Salt Lake Valley, south of the Oregon Trail, and build a settlement there. The Salt Lake Valley was outside US territory at that time and the Mormons hoped they could escape persecution there.

Reaching Omaha, 1846

Young wanted the Mormons to make their migration west in the spring of 1846 when the weather was warmer and there was grass for the livestock to eat. However, hostility in Illinois forced the Mormons to move in February. The weather was bitterly cold. The Mormon families suffered badly and could only travel slowly. It took until June for the first stage of the migration to be complete.

The Mormons congregated at Omaha at the northern starting point of the Oregon Trail. Young decided that it was now too late in the year to travel on to Salt Lake Valley. The Mormons stayed at Omaha until the following spring and endured another harsh winter.

Reaching the Great Salt Lake, 1847

In April 1847, a small party of around 150 Mormons, led by Young, set off for the Salt Lake Valley: a 2,000 km journey. This advance party was well supplied, with enough food for a year and a portable boat to help with river crossings.

Once over the South Pass in the Rocky Mountains, the Mormons left the Oregon Trail and travelled along the route used by the Donner Party. The Mormon advance party marked out the most suitable route to follow and to clear the route where needed. It also located water sources, set up river crossings and ferries, and even planted vegetable crops at places along the way.

By the time Young had reached the Salt Lake Valley in July 1847, another much larger wagon train of 1,500 Mormons was just setting off from Omaha along the same route. Thanks to the advance party, this wagon train had a clear route to follow. The second group arrived at the Salt Lake Valley in August 1847. Between 1847 and 1869, 70,000 Mormons followed the Mormon Trail to the Salt Lake Valley.

Planning the Mormon migration

Brigham Young's leadership was very important in the success of the migration. Not only did he lead the advance group to prepare the trail to the Salt Lake Valley, he also planned carefully for how the second, much larger wagon train, should make the trip.

- Before they left, Young organised a count of all the Mormons and the wagons they had available, finding that there were around 3,000 families and 2,500 wagons. This enabled him to plan the logistics of the migration: what each person needed to survive.

- Young consulted with trail guides and explorers to find out as much about the Salt Lake Valley as he could. He wanted the Mormons to be as prepared as possible to make a success of their new home.

- The migrants were divided into manageable groups, each with a leader. This meant that even if groups were separated on the journey, everyone would still know what to do.

- Young insisted on strict discipline, giving everyone a specific role. As a result, there were none of the arguments and splits that had caused the Donner Party such problems. Also, each group had the right mix of skills to help them survive.

- Young taught the migrants how to form their wagons into a circle at night. This meant they could keep their livestock safe from attack, or from getting lost.

- Regular resting places were planned along the route. This ensured that people did not exhaust their livestock, which had been a problem for the Donner Party.

Meeting the challenges of the Salt Lake Valley

The Great Salt Lake, and the land surrounding it, was a harsh, arid landscape. The lake itself was salty, and the lands surrounding it too poor to grow crops on.

Gradually, with Young's leadership, the Mormons succeeded in building a flourishing settlement. This happened because the Mormons worked together to one central plan, under strict leadership.

1 The Mormons believed that Young was God's prophet and they obeyed him completely. Young decided that the Church owned all the land: no individual owned anything. Also, everyone must work together for the good of the community.

2 The Mormons built irrigation systems from the freshwater streams that ran into the Great Salt Lake. This meant they had water to grow crops. Irrigation systems need large numbers of people to work together to build, operate and maintain them. Young had the authority to make sure this happened.

Source C

A painting by William Henry Jackson showing Mormon pioneers heading to Utah and the Salt Lake Valley in the 1850s.

Source D

A description of the Salt Lake Valley, written by one of the first settlers.

A broad and barren plain hemmed in by mountains, blistering in the burning rays of the midsummer sun. No waving fields, no swaying forests, no green meadows. But on all sides a seemingly endless waste of sagebrush – the paradise of the lizard, the cricket [grasshopper] and the rattlesnake.

3 In order that the Mormons would have all the different products they needed, new settlements were planned and each one was designed to produce particular products, such as food crops, minerals or timber. Young sent out a mix of people with the skills each settlement would need, such as blacksmiths, carpenters and millers. Each settlement had a Church leader with authority over everything.

4 New Mormon settlements spread out away from the Salt Lake Valley, into areas with more reliable water supplies. Products from these settlements (such as vegetables, flour, timber and metals) were brought back to Great Salt Lake City, founded by Young.

Activities ?

1   In pairs, plan a group migration along the Oregon Trail. Identify the challenges you will be likely to meet, and the things you need to do or take with you to meet these challenges.

2   Selecting five key events from the story of the Donner Party disaster, link them in a flow chart that explains why so many of the Donner Party died on their journey.

3   Explain the importance of planning for successful migrations: use the examples of the Donner Party and the Mormon settlement of the Great Salt Lake to add supporting detail.

Exam-style question, Section A

Explain **two** consequences of the setting up of the Oregon Trail (1836)   **8 marks**

Exam tip

A consequence is something that happens as a result of an event. Your answer should focus on consequences; there are no marks here for describing the Oregon Trail.

The development and problems of white settlement farming

The growth of settlement in Oregon and California saw big increases in the numbers crossing the Great Plains. When migrants reached their destinations in the West, many of them set up farms. They had come west to settle on land of their own – they were settlers.

In California and Oregon, farming conditions were good. Thousands of disappointed gold miners found that California's mild climate and fertile soils were excellent for growing spring wheat. By the 1850s, farmers there were producing so much wheat that California began exporting grain to Europe. There was a lot of money to be made, and farming became big business, with large farms that could afford steam-powered farm machinery and large agricultural workforces.

By the 1850s, settlement had also begun on the Great Plains. This was promoted by the US government. In 1854, the government created two new territories, Kansas and Nebraska. These territories were behind the Permanent Indian Frontier. Now the US government opened them for settlement by white Americans.

However, no whites had ever farmed the Great Plains. No one knew which crops to grow or how best to prepare the land. New settlers on the Plains faced major problems in farming the land.

Source E

This picture from the 1850s shows a Californian farmer ploughing his fields in mild November weather.

Plains problems

Low rainfall
- Half the rainfall that farmers were used to back East
- Very few rivers or streams

Few trees
- Too dry for trees away from rivers
- Plains Indians set fires to promote grass, killing saplings

Climate extremes
- Very hot summers
- Extremely cold winters
- Hailstorms, thunderstorms

Consequences for Plains farming

Too dry for crops

No rivers to transport people and products across the Plains

Not enough water for livestock

No timber for building houses

No timber for making fences

Crops shrivelled in the summer heat

Hailstorms and fires (from lightning) destroyed crops

Frequent droughts

No wood to burn for cooking and heating

Very difficult living conditions in summer and in winter

Figure 1.8 Conditions on the Great Plains led to serious difficulties for white settlement farming.

With no wood for fuel, settlers burned buffalo 'chips': buffalo dung that had dried in the Sun. Buffalo dung burned very quickly so a lot was needed to keep the house heated in winter.

On the Great Plains, water could be 300 feet down. Wells that deep were expensive to dig and winching up enough water for people, animals and crops each day was hard work.

With no trees for wood, settlers made houses out of 'sods' of earth: sod houses. Sod houses were warm and fire-proof, but were always dirty, infested with insects and started to turn into mud in heavy rain.

Families were often miles away from any other settlers, making life on the Great Plains very lonely. The nearest town could be several days of travel away.

Figure 1.9 Settlers, like this Kansas family, faced tough living and working conditions.

There were several other problems of farming on the Plains.

- Ploughing: the soil was very difficult to plough because of deep tangled grass roots. Normal ploughs broke under the strain. Farmers had to dig up the grass by hand with spades or hire a professional 'sod-buster' with a heavy plough and team of oxen, which was expensive.
- Crops: when settlers planted crops that grew well where they used to live, the crops failed because the Plains were too dry and too cold in winter.

Activity ?

Make a list of the problems the white settlers faced as they tried to farm on the Great Plains. Decide which was the most significant and why.

- Prairie* fires: after a long, hot and dry summer, the long grass of the prairie burned very easily. Prairie fires also burned crops and could kill livestock and people, too. Fires could start because of lightning strikes, a spark from a campfire or a steam train, or because Plains Indians had started a fire to encourage new grass shoots.
- Grasshoppers: some years, vast clouds of grasshoppers swept over the Plains destroying everything in their path, including crops, grass, even the wool on sheep's backs. People reported that the flying grasshoppers blacked out the Sun. There were so many that grasshopper droppings turned everything brown and polluted any water sources.

Key term

Prairie*
The large areas of flat grasslands, mostly without trees, of the Great Plains region of North America.

Extend your knowledge

Why did grasshopper outbreaks occur?

Most Great Plains locations had at least one grasshopper 'plague' per decade. The worst outbreak was in 1874, when an estimated 120 billion insects devastated over 300,000 km² of land. Grasshopper numbers increased when spring weather was hot and dry, but ploughed fields were also perfect for incubating grasshopper eggs, so the settlers were unintentionally contributing to the outbreaks.

Summary

- Different factors encouraged migration to the West: some of which were 'pushing' migrants to leave the East and some which were 'pulling' them to the West.
- The development of the Oregon Trail made migration to the West possible, but it was never easy. Sometimes it was disastrous, as with the Donner Party. Even with careful planning and organisation, it was a hard journey.
- Early settlers had a hard life on the Great Plains, because the conditions there caused many problems. No one knew how to make farming a success there.

Checkpoint

Strengthen

S1 400,000 people had followed the Oregon Trail by 1869. Which **one** of the following factors do you think was the most important in encouraging migration west along the Trail? a) the economic crisis of 1837, b) the discovery of gold in California, c) beliefs about 'Manifest Destiny'? Briefly explain your answer.

S2 Many people died following the Oregon Trail – around 20,000 between 1840 and 1860. What was the most common cause of death and how was it related to the challenges of following the Trail?

Challenge

C1 Explain why the Mormon migration was successful despite the challenges of the trip.

C2 Explain the problems facing white settlers trying to make a living farming the Great Plains.

How confident do you feel about your answers to these questions? To build your confidence, add key events to your timeline (see page 17). Practise making links between the events – for example, how could you link the Indian Appropriation Act of 1851 with the US government opening Kansas and Nebraska for settlement in 1854?

1.3 Conflict and tension

Tension between settlers and Plains Indians

Life for both settlers and Plains Indians was very challenging because of the harsh environments of the West. One bad decision or one unfortunate accident could put a group of settlers or a band of Plains Indians at great risk. This made settlers and Plains Indians very wary of possible threats.

White fear of Plains Indians

Conflict was unavoidable for Plains Indians because resources were scarce and raiding other tribes for food, horses and people was an important survival strategy. When white settlers, travelling the Oregon Trail, got caught up in these tribal conflicts, they often thought the war parties were threatening to attack them. Plains Indian attacks on migrants were rare, but white settlers scared each other with stories of attacks and misunderstood the intentions of any Plains Indian war parties they spotted.

White settlers had strongly racist views about American Indians. Most were certain that the white race was naturally superior to the American Indian race, and thought American Indians were doomed to be swept aside by whites. They felt contempt for Plains Indians who begged for supplies from them, and were angry when they stole horses and cows from them. At the same time, white settlers were very afraid that Plains Indians would attack them, scalp* the men and carry the women and children off into slavery.

Key term

Scalp*
The cutting off of the hair and skin from the top of an enemy's head to keep as a trophy and as a sign of bravery. Both the Plains Indians and whites did this.

Some settlers used Plains Indian experience and knowledge about their environment. The Mormon settlers, for example, learned a lot about how to survive in the Salt Lake Valley from studying the crops and farming methods of the Pueblo Indians. Some Plains Indians went to live among white people and learn more about white laws, religion and culture. However, this sort of interaction was not common. It was more usual for both whites and Plains Indians to have very little understanding of how the other lived and why they acted as they did. This led to mistrust.

Interpretation 1

From *The Plains Indians* (1976) by F. Haines.

When the trail to Oregon was opened to wagon trains in the early 1840s, the resulting annual flow of travellers brought critical new problems to the Indian tribes… friction between the travellers and the tribes soon built up to danger point, and minor conflicts erupted all along the way. Most problems… resulted directly from the white man's firm belief than an Indian had no rights of any kind, even in his own land.

Threats to Plains Indian food supply

The discovery of gold in California meant tens of thousands of white migrants travelled along the Oregon Trail in 1849 and 1850. This led to serious problems for Plains Indians along the Trail because the migrants disrupted buffalo hunting. The migrants killed large numbers of buffalo along the trail for meat. Also, the Plains Indian way of hunting buffalo depended on managing the herd carefully, but the migrants spooked the buffalo and caused stampedes.

Thousands of migrants also meant thousands of oxen pulling their wagons (usually a wagon had four oxen to pull it), and many migrants brought livestock with them. This meant shortages of grass in a wide area along the Oregon Trail for the animals the Plains Indians hunted, and for their horses.

Tribes did keep an eye on the migrants, therefore. The migrants often assumed that any Plains Indian warriors they saw watching them were planning to attack them. The migrants demanded that government build forts along the Oregon Trail so soldiers could crack down on any hostile Plains Indian threat.

Figure 1.10 Key events leading to the Fort Laramie Treaty (1851).

The Fort Laramie Treaty (1851)

The US government responded to the growing mistrust between whites and Plains Indians by organising a council of Plains Indian tribes from the northern Great Plains. The government's aim was for the tribes to agree to a treaty that would end conflicts between the tribes and guarantee safe access for migrants across Plains Indian lands. The negotiators also wanted to get the tribes to agree to live in fixed territories.

But, there were problems in getting agreement, which had consequences for the Treaty's success.

1 Choosing council representatives

The government negotiators wanted each tribe to name a chief who would represent the whole tribe. Plains Indian society did not work this way (see page 10). The Sioux nation, in particular, could not find a way to meet this request: it made no sense to them. Frustrated, the negotiators picked a representative from the Brulé sub-tribe called Conquering Bear. He was not a chief, but a respected warrior and member of several warrior brotherhoods.

2 Getting representatives from all the tribes

Although large numbers of Plains Indians had come, some tribes did not attend. Most of the Plains Indians who attended had no real interest in the council or its decisions (they were there for the government food and gifts).

A.k.a. the Horse Creek Treaty

Many tribes were extremely short of food and the government promise of food and gifts meant that large numbers came to the council gathering: as many as 10,000. Government negotiators were worried that they saw no buffalo as they approached Fort Laramie. When news came in that the wagons bringing the government's promised food and gifts were delayed, the negotiators moved the council to Horse Creek, 50 km east of Fort Laramie, where there were more animals to hunt. American Indian historians tend to refer to the Treaty as the Horse Creek Treaty.

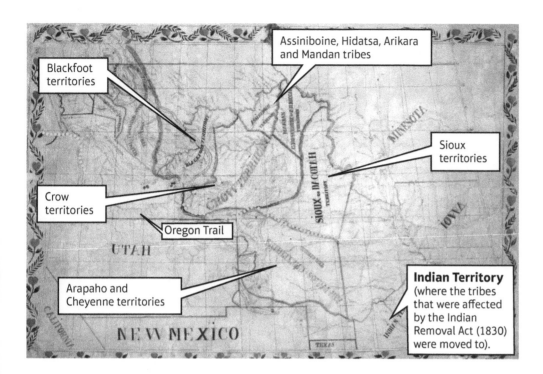

Figure 1.11 The map produced by the Fort Laramie Treaty in 1851, showing the boundaries of each tribe's territory. The approximate route of the Oregon Trail has been added and annotations to make the map clearer.

3 Agreeing boundaries

The government negotiators wanted to pin down precise boundaries to each tribe's lands to keep warring tribes apart, and they produced a map (see Figure 1.11) that was used in negotiating the Treaty. However, Plains Indians did not use the land in this way. Bands from different tribes travelled far and wide to find food, and even tribes who were enemies used the same areas of land. Bands from tribes that were allies, for example Sioux and Cheyenne tribes, often moved around together.

4 Translation difficulties

The Treaty was written in English and there were not enough translators to make sure that the representatives of all the different tribes understood it.

Treaty agreements

On 17 September 1851, the Treaty was finally signed by the council members, after over a week of negotiations. The main terms of the Treaty were:

The Plains Indians would:	The US government would:
end the fighting between the tribes allow migrants to travel through their lands in safety permit surveyors from railroad companies to enter their lands in safety	protect Plains Indians from white Americans (including migrants trying to settle on Plains Indian land)
allow the government to build roads through their lands and construct army posts pay compensation if any individuals from their tribe broke the Treaty terms (e.g. by attacking migrants)	pay the tribes an annuity (a yearly payment) of $50,000 as long as the Treaty terms were kept to

Significance of the Treaty

- The Fort Laramie Treaty did not introduce reservations for the rest of the Plains Indians, but by identifying areas of territory for each tribe, it took the first step towards reservations.
- The Treaty stated that migrants must be allowed to travel safely across the Plains. This undermined the Permanent Indian Frontier in the northern Plains (see page 17).
- The US government introduced annuities, paid in food and products, to compensate Plains Indians for allowing migrants across their lands. Plains Indian tribes now had a relationship with the government that depended on them behaving as the government wished.

Problems with the Treaty

- There was no tradition in Plains Indian society for one man to represent the wishes of the whole tribe. Although individual chiefs had signed the Treaty, each band would make its own decision whether to follow it or not.
- Not all the Plains Indian representatives understood what they had signed up to, due to translation difficulties and because of different cultural understandings about land as property. This affected what they were able to tell their tribes about the Treaty terms.
- The boundaries of the tribes' territories were not seen as meaning anything serious. When the Sioux complained that their hunting grounds were larger than those shown on the map, the government representatives said that all Plains Indians were still free to hunt in other tribes' territories.

The result of these problems was that neither side had any lasting success in sticking to the Treaty terms. Plains Indian bands continued to fight each other, which the US government saw as breaking the Treaty. Migrants did not stick to the Oregon Trail but trespassed into areas that Plains Indians viewed as strictly off limits: behaviour that should have been stopped by the US Army, but was not.

> ### Exam-style question, Section A
>
> Explain **two** consequences of the Fort Laramie Treaty (1851).
>
> **8 marks**

> ### Exam tip
>
> The question wants you to explain the results of something, in other words: what difference did it make? Use phrases such as 'as a result' or 'the effect of this was' in your answer to show the consequences of the event in the question.

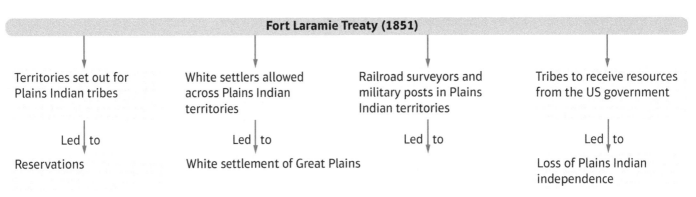

Figure 1.12 Key consequences of the Fort Laramie Treaty (1851) and their later significance.

The problems of lawlessness in early towns and settlements

Law and order

The American West is often described as being 'lawless'. This does not mean that there were not any laws. Instead, the problem was law enforcement: making people obey the laws. The official systems for law enforcement were stretched thin in the West.

Communities in the West needed law enforcement because people wanted to protect their property from theft, to be able to buy and sell things fairly, and to be able to live their lives peacefully.

The impact of mass settlement

During the early 1840s, the numbers of migrants to the West were very small. Migrant communities had to be able to rely on each other to survive, so lawless behaviour was minimal.

The situation changed with the California Gold Rush. The non-American Indian population of California in 1846 was around 8,000. By 1850, it increased to 120,000. By 1855, there were 300,000 people, including people from all over the world. This mass migration* and mass settlement* created a number of problems that the existing systems of law enforcement in California were unable to deal with.

> ### Key terms
>
> **Mass migration***
> When very large numbers of people migrate.
>
> **Mass settlement***
> When very large numbers of people come to live in an area.

The gold prospectors gathered in camps wherever gold was found. Camps grew up in days from nothing to huge tent cities of thousands of men. This was far too rapid for official state or federal law systems to be introduced. Serious problems quickly arose.

- Mining camps followed a Californian law about staking a claim*: the law set out what amount of land was fair for each prospector to claim and gave him the rights to any gold that he found there. However, 'claim jumping' was common – if a claim looked promising, other men tried to steal it.

- Mining camps attracted people looking to make money from prospectors, often by illegal methods, including 'salting a claim': scattering a few flakes of gold on a worthless claim and then conning an inexperienced migrant into buying it. Others, the road agents*, waited outside the camp to rob prospectors.

- There were also prostitutes and people selling alcohol in the mining camps. This combination often led to drunken fights between men who had formed attachments to the same woman. Because many prospectors carried guns, any violence was a threat to others in the camp.

- Prospectors came from all over the world, so mining camps mixed people of different ethnicities and from different religions. This often led to tension and triggered violence in the camps.

> ### Key terms
>
> **Claim***
> A legal declaration that someone intends to take control over an area of land.
>
> **Road agents***
> Gangs of criminals who waited in isolated spots along roads to rob travellers.

Gangs and racism

In 1849, the population of San Francisco exploded from 1,000 to 25,000. The growth continued in the 1850s, both because of new migrants arriving in California and because of changes in the Gold Rush.

- By mid-1850, many prospectors had found nothing or had 'worked out' their claim and could not find any more gold. Now professional miners, funded by rich investors, moved in to mine underground. Ordinary prospectors did not have the skills or investment to mine in this way. Instead, they became employees of the mining companies, moved to other territories to find gold, or looked for jobs (often in San Francisco).

- In 1852, a famine in China led to a huge increase in Chinese migrants coming to California: from 2,000 in 1851 to 20,000 in 1852.

Many of the thousands of disappointed prospectors who returned to San Francisco could not find work. This contributed to a crime wave in the town in 1851. Rival gangs took control of city areas. The law officers in the town were completely ineffective because of both the scale of the problem and corruption. Lawlessness reached the point where gang members would stroll into saloons, kill people, take their money, and leave.

Racism against Chinese immigrants also increased. Chinese miners were prevented from working new claims: they were only permitted to work old claims. However, by hard work, Chinese miners still made money, which led to white Americans robbing them, destroying their camps and even murdering them.

Source A

This picture from 1855 shows a California saloon filled with Chinese, European and Mexican customers.

Attempts by government and local communities to tackle lawlessness

Federal law enforcement and the sheriff

The territories of the West were under the control of the federal government. Only when a territory had a population of 60,000 could it apply to be a state, and have its own state government, laws and legal system.

The federal government decided on the laws for each territory. It also appointed a governor for the territory,

three judges to hear court cases and a US marshal* who was responsible for law enforcement. The marshal could appoint deputies to help him and could also order any man to join a posse* to hunt down lawbreakers.

Once a territory had a population of 5,000 people, communities could elect a sheriff* for their county. The sheriff had similar powers to the US marshal for this county area. Sheriffs were usually chosen for their ability to calm people down and break up fights. They had no legal training but kept order as best they could.

Key terms

US Marshal*

A police officer in charge of a district. A US marshal was a federal law officer appointed to an area.

Posse*

A group of men called together by a sheriff or marshal to help him in enforcing the law.

Sheriff*

An elected law officer with the responsibility of keeping the peace in his area and carrying out orders of a law court, such as issuing warrants, making arrests and delivering prisoners to jail.

There were some significant problems with the effectiveness of this system of law and order.

- Geography: territories were huge areas with scattered settlements. Even counties were often very large: a Kansas sheriff's county typically covered 200,000 km², for example. Before the late 1860s, horseback was the fastest way of travel, so news of trouble took a long time to reach law officers, and then it took a long time for officers to get to where they were needed. Even with deputies, there were not enough law officers for effective law enforcement.

- The federal government did not spend much on the territories, so law enforcement was badly paid. As a result, it was hard to recruit law officers and many were corrupt – accepting money from criminals to avoid arrest, or taking a cut from criminal activities.

- Because they had no legal training, sheriffs did not always act fairly, favouring their friends over other people. This injustice increased tensions.

Settling claim disputes in mining camps

Mining communities did not have easy access to a legal system of judges and courts in order to settle disputes. So, mining communities got together to agree and write down the rules that would govern mining in their district. A recorder was chosen to record all the claims that were made and who had claimed them. The community also created its own court, with a respected community member chosen to judge the disputes. Juries were often appointed as well.

Vigilance committees

The crime wave in San Francisco in 1851 produced a new form of law enforcement: the vigilance committee – better known as vigilantes*. Although San Francisco had a legal system, many townspeople believed that the courts were corrupt. This was unacceptable to the rich businessmen of San Francisco – those with the most to lose. They organised a vigilance committee of around 200 men.

The committee captured suspected criminals, tried them and punished those that they found guilty. In 1851, 89 suspects were captured and tried. Around half were found not guilty, a quarter were deported, 15 were handed over to law enforcement officers and the rest were hanged. Once the committee felt that law and order had been restored, it disbanded itself.

Key term

Vigilantes*

A group of ordinary citizens who punish suspected lawbreakers themselves instead of relying on the official justice system (usually because it is inadequate).

The idea of vigilance committees spread rapidly through the mining camps in the West. Miners were sick of road agents, horse thieves and swindlers, but the mining courts settled disputes about claims and they had no power to tackle criminal behaviour. Some communities elected sheriffs, but often they were unable to tackle the lawlessness on their own.

Once vigilance committees had been organised, they were very effective. They identified their suspects, tried them and, often, hanged them. Warnings would appear around the camp so that any remaining troublemakers knew to clear out.

A problem with the vigilance committees was that there was not often a fair trial: a person's guilt was usually decided before they were captured. This often led to the lynching* of suspects. However, the main problem with vigilance committees was that they had a tendency to use their power to settle scores, and some went on to be worse than the criminals they hanged.

Key term

Lynching*

This occurs when a group of people takes the law into their own hands and executes someone they suspect of a crime (usually by hanging).

Source B

This picture, from 1892, shows a lynch mob coming to hang a murderer in a mining settlement. It is a reproduction of a painting made in 1848.

Dealing with racist crimes

Racist attacks increased as a result of mass settlement in California, especially against American Indians and Chinese migrants. Unfortunately, the state government was also racist. White Americans were encouraged to murder Californian Indians and laws were passed that discriminated against Chinese migrants. California's state government passed a law that taxed Chinese miners more than the US citizens, and another law saying that Chinese people could not be witnesses in court (the same was true for black Americans and American Indians).

Activity ?

Using Figure 1.13 to help you, identify three factors that encouraged communities in the West to set up vigilance committees rather than rely on state or federal law enforcement.

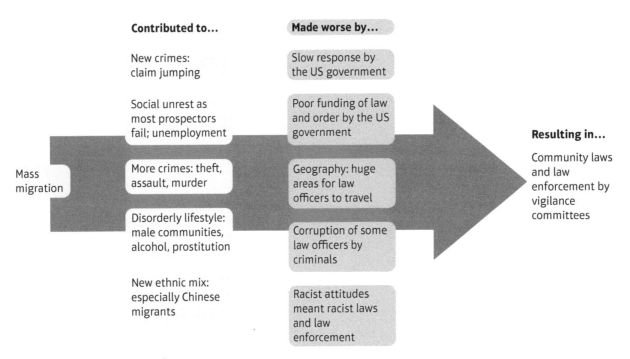

Figure 1.13 Consequences of mass migration.

Summary

- The growing number of settlers moving on to the Plains led to conflict between settlers and Plains Indians.
- The Fort Laramie Treaty (1851) involved promises being made by both the Plains Indians and the government.
- Law and order was difficult to enforce in the early towns and settlements. In some settlements, a lack of government help meant local communities tried tackling lawlessness themselves.

Checkpoint

Strengthen

S1 What size population did a territory need to reach before sheriffs could be elected there?

S2 Describe how a vigilance committee (vigilante group) tackled lawlessness.

Challenge

C1 Suggest two ways in which a lack of understanding of Plains Indian culture and traditions caused increased tensions between white settlers and Plains Indians.

C2 Why was the geography of the West significant in making law and order difficult to enforce?

How confident do you feel about your answers to these questions? One way you could boost your understanding it to write down the key terms from the topic and see how many connections you can make between them. For example, what connects: 'sheriff' and 'posse'?

Recap: The early settlement of the West, c1835–c1862

35

Recall quiz

1 Give three uses of the buffalo by the Plains Indians.

2 In 1848, the USA gained new territories in the West due to its victory over which country?

3 Identify two problems for settlers on the Plains due to the lack of trees.

4 In what year was the Indian Appropriations Act passed by the US government?

5 What happened in 1837 that acted to 'push' some white settlers from the East to the West?

6 Identify a (bad) decision that led to the Donner Party disaster.

7 Identify three reasons why the Mormons were able to survive the challenges of early settlement-building in the Great Salt Lake region.

8 'The Fort Laramie Treaty of 1851 created reservations for the Plains Indians of the northern Plains.' Is that statement true or false?

9 Write a definition of 'Manifest Destiny'.

10 What did the US government hope to achieve by creating a Permanent Indian Frontier?

Activities ?

1 Figure 1.14 shows a map of the USA in 1861. There are two arrows on it, representing pressures on the Plains Indians from the East and also from the West. Redraw the map and add text to the two arrows explaining the factors putting pressure on the Plains Indians in the period 1835 to 1862.

2 Thinking about everything you have learned in this chapter, which one event would you argue was the most significant for the settlement of the American West in the period from 1835 to 1862? Explain the choice you have made.

Exam-style question, Section A

Explain **two** of the following:

- The importance of the Oregon Trail for the early settlement of the West.
- The importance of the Indian Appropriations Act (1851) for the way of life of the Plains Indians.
- The importance of the development of new mining towns for law and order in the early West. **16 marks**

Exam tip

Although three bullet points are listed, the question only asks you to pick two of them for your answer. You should pick the two you can answer best and write two separate answers for this question. Pay careful attention to what exactly you are being asked to explain: the second part of each bullet point gives you the specific focus of the question.

Figure 1.14 A map of the USA in 1861 showing the rough locations of some of the larger Plains Indian tribes.

States
Territories
Sioux Plains Indian tribe

Writing historically: building information

When you are asked to write an explanation or analysis, you need to provide as much detailed information as possible.

Learning outcomes

By the end of this lesson, you will understand how to:

- use relative clauses to add clear and detailed information to your writing
- use noun phrases in apposition to add clear and detailed information to your writing.

Definitions

Relative clause: a clause that adds information or modifies a noun, linked with a relative pronoun, e.g. 'who', 'that', 'which', 'where', 'whose'.

Noun phrase in apposition: two noun phrases, positioned side-by-side, the second adding information to the first, e.g. [1] 'San Francisco, [2] the port city where many migrants arrived in California, grew rapidly between 1849 and 1855.'

How can I add detail to my writing?

Look at a sentence from the response below to this exam-style question:

> Explain the importance of the discovery of gold in California (1848) for the settlement of the American West. **(8 marks)**

> *Many of the miners, who had failed to find gold, settled in California as farmers.*

The main clause is highlighted in yellow. The relative pronoun is underlined. The relative clause is highlighted in purple.

This noun phrase is modified by this **relative clause**: it provides more information about the miners.

1. How could you restructure the sentence above using two separate sentences?

2. Why do you think the writer chose to structure these sentences using a main clause and a relative clause instead of writing them as two separate sentences?

Now look at these four sentences taken from the same response:

> *Gold was discovered in 1848. This was enough to make thousands of people attempt the journey west. They made the journey overland and by sea. It was dangerous and difficult.*

3. How effectively is this information expressed? Write a sentence or two explaining your answer.

4. How could you improve the written expression in the answer above, using relative pronouns?

   a. Rewrite the sentences, using relative pronouns to link all the information in **one** sentence.

   b. Now rewrite the sentence using relative pronouns to link the information in **two** sentences.

   c. Which version do you prefer? Is the information most clearly and fluently expressed in one, two or four sentences? Write a sentence or two explaining your choice.

How can I add detail to my writing in different ways?

You can also add detail to a sentence using a **noun phrase in apposition**.

Compare these sentences:

> *Migration to the West, which was a long and dangerous journey, was attempted by thousands of people in search of a fortune in gold.*

This uses a relative clause to add information clearly and briefly.

> *Migration to the West, a long and dangerous journey, was attempted by thousands of people in search of a fortune in gold.*

This uses a noun phrase in apposition to add the same information even more clearly and briefly.

5. How could you combine the information in the pairs of sentences below using a noun phrase in apposition?

> *San Francisco became the largest city on the West Coast in 1849. It had been a small settlement before the gold rush.*
>
> *The mass migration of 1849 showed that settling in the West was achievable. It had seemed very difficult before then.*

Did you notice?

6. If you remove the relative clause or the noun phrase in apposition from the sentences above, they both still make sense. They are also both separated from the rest of the sentence with commas. Can you explain why? Write a sentence or two explaining your ideas.

Improving an answer

Look at the extract below from another response to the exam question on the previous page:

> *The Gold Rush led to a sudden influx of migrants to California. It was a decisive factor in making the West seem like an attractive place to live. The rapidly rising population of miners led to the creation and growth of towns. The miners all needed food, shops, transport and equipment. This added to the growth of towns as shopkeepers and traders also settled in them. The shopkeepers and traders provided the miners with what they needed.*

7. a. Rewrite the information in the answer above, making it as clear and brief as possible. You could use:

- relative clauses

- nouns in apposition.

b. Look carefully at your response to Question 7a. Are all your sentences easy to read and understand, or are some of them too long and confusing? If so, try re-writing them to make their meaning as clear as possible.

02 | Development of the Plains, c1862–c1876

The American Civil War (1861–65) was between the northern states and the southern states of the USA. The southern states had blocked plans for government help in developing the West. When the southern states withdrew from the USA during the Civil War, it cleared the way for new legislation to build railroads right across the USA, from east to west. When the Civil War ended, a new wave of settlers poured onto the Plains.

The railroads brought new settlers to the Plains and also supplied them with products made in the USA's big cities. Meanwhile, in the southern state of Texas, cattlemen were desperate to find ways to sell their cattle to buyers in the cities in the North and East of the USA, where demand for meat was very high. The new railroads were the key to this, and the cattle industry boomed into a 'beef bonanza'.

Ranching also began on the Plains, with enormous numbers of cattle roaming the 'open range', guarded and rounded up by cowboys living and working on the ranches.

As the development of the Plains increased, so too did conflicts over how the Plains were to be used: conflicts between homesteaders and ranchers, between the large ranches and the small ranches and, in particular, conflicts between Plains Indians and the new inhabitants of the Plains. The government continued to encourage Plains Indians to move to reservations where they would be 'protected', but multiple problems with the reservation system and continuing tensions over routes across Plains Indian lands led to 'Indian wars' between Plains Indian tribes and the US Army.

Learning outcomes

By the end of this chapter, you will:

- understand how the end of the American Civil War, government policies and the building of railroads all boosted the settlement of the Plains
- understand what caused the cattle industry to boom in the West, and how changes in the cattle industry affected the life of cowboys
- understand the impacts of the development of the Plains on the Plains Indians, and the conflicts that resulted with the US Army.

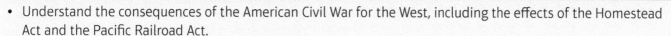

2.1 The development of settlement in the West

Before the 1860s, the California Gold Rush had been the main factor bringing large numbers of migrants to the West. Many travelled by sea, but two-thirds crossed the USA along the Oregon Trail. After the end of the American Civil War, new factors contributed to a new wave of settlement in the West as people moved to start a new life as independent farmers on the Plains. Each was significant in its own right, but there were also strong connections between many factors. US government policy and the Civil War were particularly strongly connected.

The significance of the American Civil War on the development of the West

In 1861, seven southern states left the USA (soon joined by four more) and set up their own Confederacy, which triggered the Civil War. After four years of fighting, the Union (what was left of the USA after the Confederate states left) defeated the Confederacy and the Confederate states rejoined the USA. By the time the war ended in 1865, over 600,000 Americans had died and another 400,000 were wounded. Many of the southern states were devastated by the war.

After the Civil War the US government set about rebuilding the USA. This involved repairing the enormous devastation through the South, and granting citizenship to former African American slaves.

The economic problems and social changes in the South after the war led to many people looking to start a new life in the West. Many of these people were ex-soldiers and former slaves. Settling in the West after the Civil War was easier due to laws passed by the US government during the war.

Government support for settlement in the West during the civil war

Before the Civil War began, the US government was made up of representatives of southern states and representatives of northern states. North and South both had different ideas about the West.

- Southern states relied on slave labour for their plantation farms. They wanted slavery to be legal in new states in the West, as it was legal in the South.
- Northern states wanted new states in the West to be free of slavery. Instead of large plantations owned by rich whites and worked by slaves, northerners wanted family farms worked by free, independent individuals.

When the southern states left the USA in 1861 to set up the Confederacy, it meant the US government was now controlled by the northern states. In 1862, free from opposition from southern states the US government passed two laws that had huge significance for the West.

- **The Homestead Act** (May 1862) – aimed at settling the West with individual farms, owned and worked by free men and women.
- **The Pacific Railroad Act** (July 1862) – aimed at developing connections between the new lands of the West and the northern industrial cities.

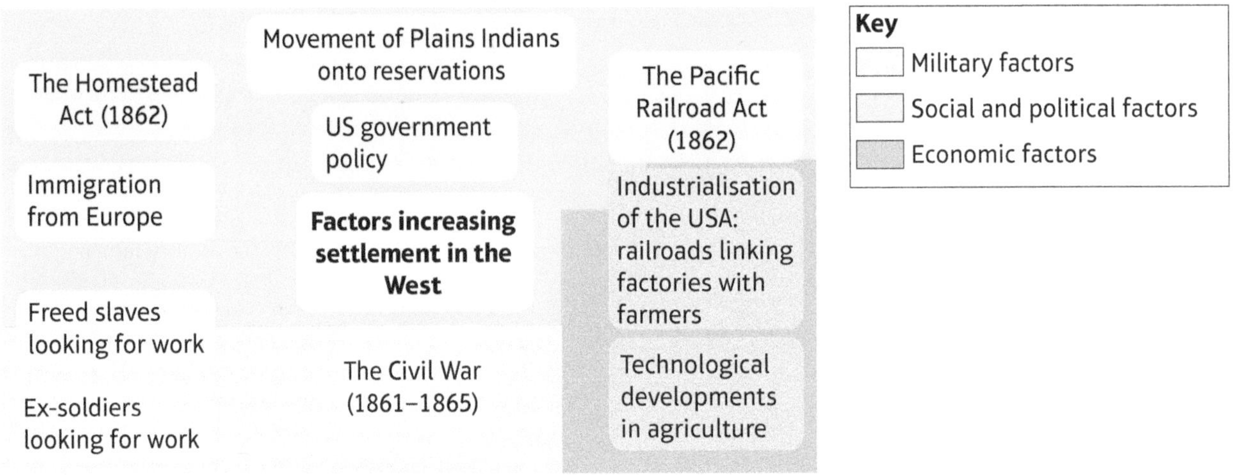

The Homestead Act (1862)

Immigration from Europe

Movement of Plains Indians onto reservations

US government policy

Factors increasing settlement in the West

Freed slaves looking for work

Ex-soldiers looking for work

The Civil War (1861–1865)

The Pacific Railroad Act (1862)

Industrialisation of the USA: railroads linking factories with farmers

Technological developments in agriculture

Key
- Military factors
- Social and political factors
- Economic factors

Figure 2.1 Key factors in the new wave of settlement in the West, 1862–76.

The Homestead Act (1862)

The Homestead Act promoted the settlement of the West. It provided incentives for people to take up unclaimed land in the West and build a new life there.

Before 1862, the government had tried to encourage settlement of its Western territories by dividing public land (owned by the government) into sections of 640 acres (1 acre = 4,047 m^2) that were then sold at $1 per acre. This was too expensive for most ordinary families.

The Homestead Act fixed this problem by making the plots of land smaller and essentially giving them away to ordinary people.

- The plots were 160-acre 'homesteads'. A homestead meant a family house and enough land to support the family. (People taking up homesteads were called homesteaders.)
- It cost just $10 to register a claim to a homestead plot – called 'filing a claim'.

The US government did not want all the land in the West to be bought up by a few rich landowners. It wanted to encourage the settlement of the West by lots of individual farmers. Thousands of small farmers all paying property taxes would give a big boost to the US economy. As a result:

- Anyone could file a claim as long as they were the head of a family or single and over 21 (or younger than 21 but an ex-soldier). This meant ex-slaves and single women could file claims. Anyone intending to become a US citizen could file a claim (though American Indians could not).
- Anyone filing a claim had then to live on the land and work the land themselves. There were limits on how many claims one person could take up. The government wanted to prevent businessmen snapping up lots of land cheaply under the scheme and then selling it on at a profit.
- Once someone had lived on the land for five years, built a house and planted five acres of crops, they could pay $30 and own their homestead outright (this was called 'proving up').

The significance of the Homestead Act

Achievements

- By 1876, over six million acres of government land had successfully become homesteads.

- The Homestead Act ensured that parts of the Great Plains were being settled for the first time. Eventually, 80 million acres of public land were settled as a direct consequence of the Homestead Act. The biggest success was in Nebraska: nearly half of all settled land here was homestead land and Nebraska's population growth resulted in it becoming a state in 1867.

- The Homestead Act was important in encouraging immigration from Europe. By 1875, more than half of Nebraska's population of 123,000 were recent immigrants and their children.

Limitations

- Only 13 million acres of claims had been 'proved up' by 1884; 24 million acres by 1900.

- Although 80 million acres was eventually homesteaded, this was out of a total of 500 million acres of public land (16%). The government granted far more land to the railroads – 300 million acres – and sold the rest of it for higher prices, often to cattle ranchers.

- Many more homesteads were formed by people buying land from the railroad companies (and through a form of squatting* called pre-emption) than were proven up through the Homestead Act.

- 60% of homestead claims were never proved up, often because of the challenges of farming the Plains.

- Despite the government's intention that the Homestead Act would produce lots of individual family farms, rich landowners were able to use it to get more land very cheaply. For example, big ranch owners would make all their employees file claims and then hand over the rights to the land to the ranch owner.

- The Homestead Act also allowed people to buy their claim for $1.25 per acre once they had ploughed one acre of it and lived there for six months. As a result, many people filed claims in order to sell it on at a profit. The consequence was that the family that eventually ended up farming the land had usually paid someone for it rather than proving it up by the Homestead Act.

Key term

Squatting*
Settling land without any legal right to do this.

Activitiy

Study Source A, an advert to encourage people to settle as homesteaders in Nebraska.

a   Did the Homestead Act provide 'lands for the landless' and 'homes for the homeless'?

b   Why did the government 'almost donate' (i.e. gave away free) millions of acres in the Homestead Act?

c   Explain one connection between the Homestead Act and the Civil War.

d   Why do you think the advert mentions that the land on offer is 'near some railroad'?

Source A

Part of a pamphlet from 1869 advertising the opportunities for homesteaders in Nebraska.

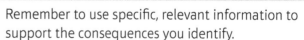

Exam-style question, Section A

Explain **two** consequences of the Homestead Act (1862).   **8 marks**

Exam tip

Remember to use specific, relevant information to support the consequences you identify.

The Pacific Railroad Act (1862)

The Pacific Railroad Act provided the incentive for transcontinental railroad building. The railroads made migration to the West much easier and quicker, they promoted the development of towns, they boosted the sale of land to settlers, and they enabled the industrial centres of the North to connect to the developing agricultural areas of the West.

The First Transcontinental Railroad

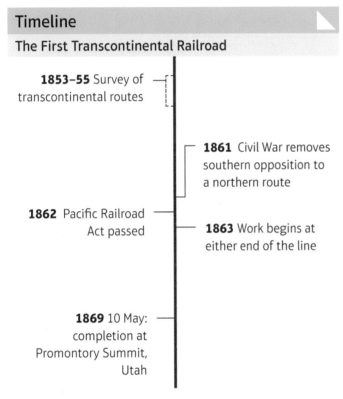

Timeline

The First Transcontinental Railroad

1853–55 Survey of transcontinental routes

1861 Civil War removes southern opposition to a northern route

1862 Pacific Railroad Act passed

1863 Work begins at either end of the line

1869 10 May: completion at Promontory Summit, Utah

There were two main problems against building a railroad to connect the eastern and western halves of the USA before 1862. First, was the enormous difficulty and cost of building a 2,000 km railroad, especially through the mountains of the West, which meant no private company would risk it. Second, was disagreement between northern and southern states. The North wanted to connect California with its big industrial cities, like Chicago. The southern states recognised that this would disadvantage them and wanted a southern route.

Like the Homestead Act, the Pacific Railroad Act was a consequence of the southern states leaving the Union in 1861, which handed control of federal government to the northern states. In 1862, the railroad network in the North was extensive, but reached only as far west as the Missouri River. The government selected a route that went from Sacramento, California, to Omaha, Nebraska. From Omaha, the First Transcontinental Railroad would link up with the existing eastern railroad network.

The Pacific Railroad Act split the job of building the First Transcontinental Railroad between two companies: the **Union Pacific** and the **Central Pacific**. The Union Pacific started in Omaha and built its track westwards. The Central Pacific started in Sacramento and built eastwards. In order to make the job possible and profitable for the two companies, the Pacific Railroad Act committed the US government to:

- 'extinguishing' any rights Plains Indians might have to land along the route
- loaning each company $16,000 for every mile of track they laid ($48,000 for mountain areas)
- granting each company large sections of public land along the railroad for them to sell.

As well as funding the building of the First Transcontinental Railroad, the Pacific Railroad Act also set up the first transcontinental electric telegraph: the route of this ran along the railroad tracks.

In all, the government gave the two railroad companies 45 million acres of free land and loaned them over $61 million (for comparison, the US government paid Russia $7.2 million for Alaska in 1867). Despite this, both companies nearly went bust: partly because of the challenges of this enormous engineering feat and partly because the Union Pacific company was caught charging the government more than it spent in order to make more money for its investors.

The railroads and settlement of the West

The railroad companies used marketing to encourage settlers to buy their land grants. They laid on special trips to show possible buyers the attractions of the area, organised loans to help people buy the land, and sent successful settlers on tours to recruit new customers.

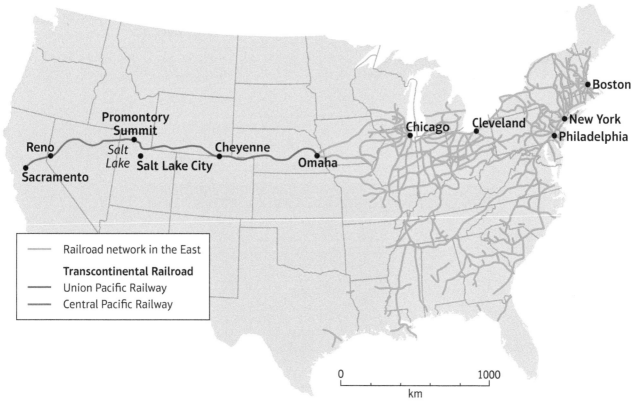

Figure 2.2 The route of the First Transcontinental Railroad.

Each railroad company had a Bureau of Immigration to persuade people from foreign countries to settle on the Plains. One agent claimed to have persuaded 10,000 Scandinavians to settle in Nebraska, while another, C.B. Schmidt, was directly responsible for 60,000 Germans emigrating to Kansas. By 1880, the railroad companies had settled 200 million acres in the West. They were more influential than the Homestead Act in encouraging settlement because they had more land to sell, better marketing and because people wanted to settle near the railroad.

Activities ?

1 You are working for a railroad company's advertising department. Design a poster to encourage poor farmers from Europe to come and settle on a homestead on the Plains.

2 The numbers of migrants using the Oregon Trail declined sharply after 1869. Explain how this was connected to the First Transcontinental Railroad.

Source B

An 1872 advert for land for sale by the Burlington and Missouri River Railroad Company.

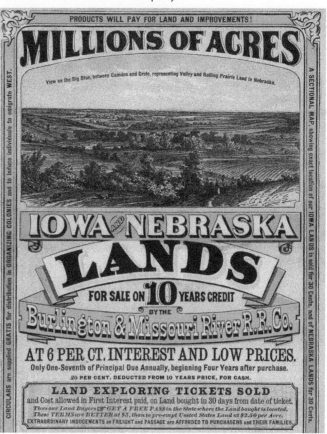

43

Impacts of the railroads

Railroads had major impacts on many different aspects of the development of settlement in the West. These impacts are summarised in Figure 2.3 and are explored in the rest of this chapter.

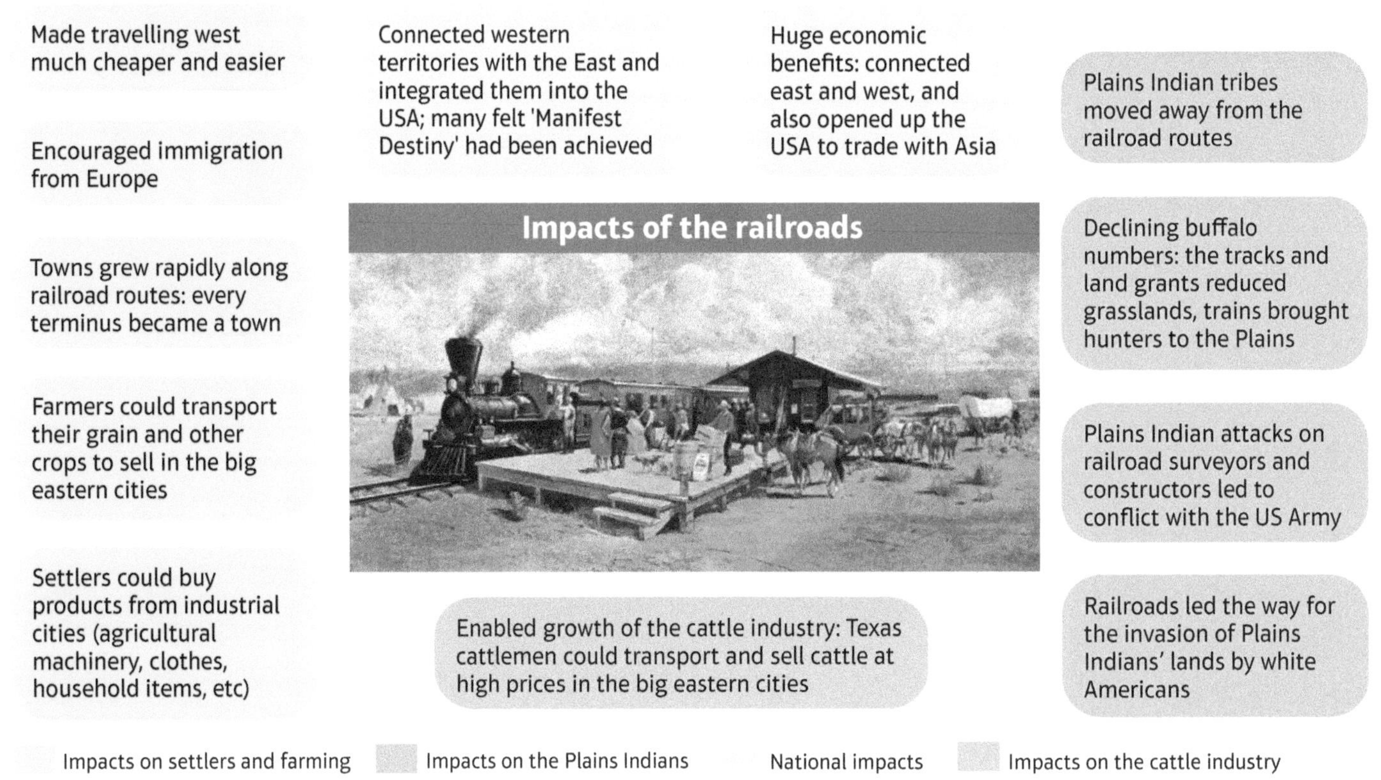

Made travelling west much cheaper and easier

Encouraged immigration from Europe

Towns grew rapidly along railroad routes: every terminus became a town

Farmers could transport their grain and other crops to sell in the big eastern cities

Settlers could buy products from industrial cities (agricultural machinery, clothes, household items, etc)

Connected western territories with the East and integrated them into the USA; many felt 'Manifest Destiny' had been achieved

Huge economic benefits: connected east and west, and also opened up the USA to trade with Asia

Plains Indian tribes moved away from the railroad routes

Declining buffalo numbers: the tracks and land grants reduced grasslands, trains brought hunters to the Plains

Plains Indian attacks on railroad surveyors and constructors led to conflict with the US Army

Railroads led the way for the invasion of Plains Indians' lands by white Americans

Impacts of the railroads

Enabled growth of the cattle industry: Texas cattlemen could transport and sell cattle at high prices in the big eastern cities

Impacts on settlers and farming ■ Impacts on the Plains Indians ■ National impacts ■ Impacts on the cattle industry

Figure 2.3 Major impacts of the railroads on the development of settlement in the West.

Tackling the problems of homesteading

The promotional marketing for homesteads minimised the challenges of farming the Plains (pages 24–25). The railroad companies even claimed that the steam from their trains would encourage more rain to fall on the Plains.

Homesteaders needed savings of between $800 and $1,000 to get started: for ploughing fields, digging a well, buying horses and farming equipment, and building a house and outbuildings. If a lack of rain then meant no crops to sell, homesteaders could quickly run out of money.

The effects of the railroads

The railroad did make homestead life easier as:

- homesteaders could visit relations much more easily and cheaply than before, which reduced the isolation of homestead life

- homesteaders could order manufactured products that made life easier – most were ordered from the Chicago-based 'Sears Roebuck & Company' catalogue, then transported by rail to the nearest railroad station

- towns sprang up at regular distances along the railroads, which gave homesteaders a place to meet each other, compare farming ideas, sell crops and buy products, and access entertainment.

These improvements to homesteader life meant that more homesteaders came to the Plains to settle.

New inventions

The combination of large numbers of settlers and major farming challenges was very attractive for the USA's inventors and manufacturers. If solutions to the problems of farming in the West could be found, then a lot of money could be made. The table below shows three important inventions.

As new inventions were improved, became cheaper and proved their worth to farmers, they began to be used all across the West. Before 1876, however, they were still 'in development' and were not widely used (see Chapter 3).

	1854: 'self-governing' windmill, 1870 steel blades	1874: barbed wire	1875: sulky plow
Purpose	Windmills were used to pump water out of the ground to help farmers irrigate their land and make it more fertile for crops.	Barbed wire was used to fence off crops to protect them from livestock and other animals.	Strong ploughs were used to plough up the tough weeds and prairie grass on the Great Plains.
Advantage	Halladay's windmill (or wind pump) could pump water out of quite deep wells (30 feet) and, in 1870, steel blades meant the windmills could stand up better to the strong prairie winds.	Much cheaper than buying in timber for fences, and much more effective at blocking livestock than smooth-wire fencing.	A very strong, easy-to-operate ride-on steel plough that made ploughing up tough weeds and prairie grass much easier. 50,000 sulky plows were sold in the first six years of production.
Problems	Not powerful enough to pump up water from very deep wells (more than 30 feet) and needed constant maintenance. It was not until the 1880s that these problems were overcome: see page 72.	Not widely used until after 1880. Early types broke and rusted and in 1874, it was ten times more expensive than in the 1880s.	Six times as many 'walking' ploughs were sold in the same period – these were cheaper and farmers understood them. Early sulkies were unstable and could tip up.

Extend your knowledge

Barbed wire

Barbed wire had an enormous impact on the West, because of laws requiring farmed land to be separated from roaming cattle by fences, and laws stating that railroad companies were responsible for any accidents on their lines if tracks had not been fenced off. Joseph Glidden, the 'Father of Barbed Wire', became a millionaire.

Activity ?

For each one of the three inventions shown here, identify the problem of farming in the West that they were designed to overcome. Look back at pages 24–25 for the problems.

New crops

In 1873, railroad agents succeeded in persuading a religious community called the Mennonites to move from Russia to the Great Plains. The Mennonites were tough, independent-minded farmers who had farmed grasslands in Russia with a similar climate to the Great Plains. Mennonites discovered that 'Turkey Red' wheat grew well on their Kansas farms. Soon farmers with good land were able to export grain, which was a major boost to settlement on the Plains.

The Timber Culture Act (1873)

Although 160 acres of land was sufficient for a family farm in the East, where rainfall was higher than in the West, it was not sufficient for successful farming on the Great Plains. The Timber Culture Act allowed a homesteader to claim a further 160 acres if she or he promised to plant trees on a quarter of it. Trees were important because they could:

- act as a 'wind break': slow down the Great Plains winds to shelter crops from damage
- provide settlers with timber for building houses, fences and furniture, and for repairing equipment
- provide settlers with fuel.

The Timber Culture Act was a correction to the Homestead Act that aimed to reduce the high rate of failure of homesteads in the Great Plains. 16 million acres had been claimed under this Act by 1878, adding 50% more land to that claimed under the Homestead Act (though only a third of this land was ever 'proven up'). The majority of claims were in Dakota Territory, Kansas and Nebraska, but unfortunately most of the trees planted died because there was not enough water for them. It was only in the state of Minnesota where large increases in tree cover took place. People also exploited loopholes in the Act to claim land that they had no intention of settling: after waiting for a few years for the price of land to rise, they sold their claims for a profit. The Act was heavily criticised for this.

Problems of law and order
Impact of the railroads – 'Hell on Wheels'

The new towns created by the railroads were lawless places at first – they were known as 'Hell on Wheels'. The most lawless railroad towns of all were the 'cow towns'. After long weeks herding cattle to these towns, cowboys would load the cows onto railroad wagons and then be paid their wages. The cowboys would then go out celebrating, which could lead to trouble.

Abilene was a cow town in Kansas. Its population boomed from 500 to 7,000 once the railroad reached it in 1867 (see page 50). Lawlessness boomed, too. By 1870, many of the residents were desperate. Cowboys were regularly having gunfights, there were murders and the cowboy pay-day celebrations had attracted saloons and brothels to the town; along with gamblers, swindlers, prostitutes and outlaws. The lawlessness was too much for local residents to control by themselves. When the town constructed a jail in 1870, cowboys immediately tore it down again. A sign banning the carrying of guns in the town was shot so full of holes that the words could no longer be read.

In 1870, the town's leaders hired Thomas Smith as town marshal. He issued a ban on carrying guns, and established a forceful reputation, using his boxing skills to knock out cowboys who disobeyed. He was able to enforce his gun ban quite successfully, but by November of 1870, he was shot and then killed with an axe while trying to arrest a suspected murderer. His murderers were caught and given long sentences in prison.

Abilene returned to lawlessness again until April 1871, when 'Wild Bill' Hickok was appointed town marshal. Hickok commanded fear and respect among the cowboys, but he did very little to enforce the law, spending all his time gambling in the saloons. By the end of the year, the town leaders sacked Hickok and decided the only way to end the lawlessness was to stop the cowboys and their herds from coming to the town.

Impact of the Civil War

The Civil War (1861–65) added significantly to the potential for trouble in the West because of army deserters* and because of the arrival of large numbers of ex-soldiers in the West after the war.

Key term

Deserters*

Soldiers who run away from the army. Deserting was a criminal offence.

Gangs of outlaws were often made up of former soldiers. Many of these men were traumatised by the war and were unable to find work in peacetime. Outlaws who were former Confederate soldiers might also be resentful towards the victorious US government. In many places in the West, law enforcement was still too weak to control outlaw gangs, and the gangs terrified local people and law officers into doing what they said.

The Reno Gang

The Reno Gang were a group of Civil War deserters, con-men and thieves who terrorised communities in the West. They also bribed local law officers to avoid arrest.

In 1866, the Reno Gang carried out a train robbery, breaking open a safe to get away with $16,000. The owners of the safe hired detectives from the Pinkerton National Detective Agency to hunt down the gang. The detectives caught John Reno, but the gang struck again in 1867 and 1868. A fourth train robbery netted the gang $96,000. Their fifth attempt saw one member of the gang captured and he gave up the rest of the gang in return for a reduced sentence. However, when the Pinkertons used this information to arrest the gang, a vigilance committee arrived, took the men and lynched them.

Extend your knowledge

The Pinkertons

Pinkerton's National Detective Agency was formed in 1850 and acted as a private law enforcement agency. The Pinkertons were used extensively in the West to track down outlaws and bring them to justice.

Source C

A photo showing Pinkerton agents. The man sitting down is the son of Alfred Pinkerton, who founded Pinkerton's National Detective Agency in 1850.

Lawlessness and the West

Lawlessness in towns happened when big social changes, like a booming population or a civil war, meant that local communities could not enforce the law themselves and state or federal government lacked the resources to help. Victims of lawlessness had to meet force with force: either by hiring a tough sheriff or town marshal to keep the peace, or by hiring a private police force, like the Pinkertons. (See Section 3.2 in Chapter 3 for more on federal government influence on law and order.)

However, most places in the West were not lawless. Even in the wildest cow towns, murders were rare. Because life was hard and many people were struggling to make a living, theft was common. But because no one could afford to lose property in this way, local communities tried hard to catch and punish thieves.

THINKING
HISTORICALLY **Cause and Consequence (2c)**

Far-reaching consequences

Most events have multiple consequences. Their impact can often be felt in many different 'strands' of history. The American Civil War (1861–65) was a significant event in the history of the West that had consequences in several different areas.

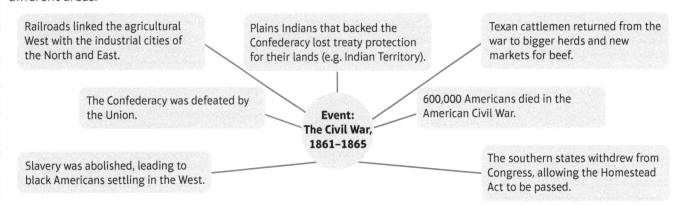

1 How many consequences have been identified? Do you think any have been missed?

2 Suggest a category (e.g. political, social, cultural, economic) for each consequence.

3 Which of these consequences do you think the two sides in the Civil War might have had in mind when the war first started?

4 Which of the consequences might the historian writing a history of the American West **not** refer to? Explain your answer.

5 Write one historical question about the Civil War that might require the historian to know about all these consequences in order to answer it well.

Summary

- A new wave of settlement in the West followed the Civil War, aided by the government's Homestead Act (1862) and Pacific Railroad Act (1862), and by the railroad companies.
- The new wave of settlers started to benefit from new methods of farming the Plains.
- The new wave of settlement following the Civil War and the expansion of railroads into the West brought new problems of law and order to some areas.

Checkpoint

Strengthen

S1 Why did the US government want homesteaders to buy land rather than big landowners? Explain the significance of the Pacific Railroad Act (1862) for the settlement of the West.

S2 Identify the connections between: a) the Civil War b) the railroads c) problems of law and order in the West.

Challenge

C1 Which of the two government incentives, the Homestead Act (1862) or the Pacific Railroad Act (1862), do you think had the greatest impact on the settlement of the West? Explain your answer.

C2 Study Figure 2.1 at the start of this chapter. Write a sentence to explain the importance of each box in the diagram to the development of settlement in the West.

How confident do you feel about your answers to these questions? Continuing your American West timeline will help: now you can start to add some key events for the period 1862–76.

2.2 Ranching and the cattle industry

Learning outcomes

- Understand the growth of the cattle industry after the Civil War.
- Understand the significance of this growth, including the effects on cowboys and the rivalry between ranchers and homesteaders.

In the 1870s, the West was developing due to the impact of settlers spreading westwards along the railroad tracks to states and territories west of the Missouri River, and due to prospectors spreading eastwards through the Rocky Mountains looking for gold. The growth of the cattle industry also impacted on the development of the West: spreading up from the South, from Texas.

Timeline
The growth of the cattle industry

1836 Start of Texan cattle drives to Missouri (Shawnee Trail)

1855 Quarantine law in Missouri blocks Texas cattle

1861 Iliff buys a herd of cows and fattens them on the Plains in Colorado Territory

1861–65 The American Civil War – longhorn cattle numbers boom

1866 Kansas farmers prevent a drive from Texas to Sedalia, Missouri

1866 Goodnight and Loving drive cattle to Fort Sumner, New Mexico

1867 McCoy establishes the first cow town, Abilene, Kansas

1868 Goodnight–Loving Trail extended to Cheyenne, Wyoming

1870 Iliff's ranch extends to 16,000 acres of open range

1867–72 A total of three million cattle driven along the Chisolm Trail to Abilene

The Texan cattle industry before the Civil War

When Texas became independent from Mexico in 1836, Texans took over the Mexican cattle industry and the skills and traditions of the **vaqueros** – horse-riding cattle herders that the Texans named cowboys.

The Texan cowboys herded the cows on long drives*, along cattle trails* across the South to New Orleans and also up through Missouri to towns like Sedalia and St Louis. From Sedalia, the cattle were transported to the big cities of the North.

A cattle disease, known as Texas fever, had major impacts on the cattle drives. If a Missouri cow mixed with Texas cattle, or even ate from grass that the Texas cattle had travelled over, they often caught Texas fever. It was almost always fatal. As a result, farmers in both Missouri and southern Kansas were strongly opposed to Texan cattle drives across their land.

In 1855, Missouri farmers formed vigilance committees to block the drives. Then, a quarantine* law was passed preventing infected Texan cattle from entering Missouri. Kansas passed a similar law in 1859. Texans were looking for alternative routes for cattle drives when the Civil War interrupted everything.

Key terms

Long drives*
Herding cattle (or other animals) over long distances.

Cattle trails*
Routes used for driving cattle: these needed to have easy access to both grass and water.

Quarantine*
Keeping an animal that might be diseased away from other animals to stop the spread of disease.

Growth of the cattle industry after the war

After the Civil War ended in 1865, beef was in great demand in the big industrial cities of the North. In 1865 a cow was worth $40 in Chicago, where industrialised meat-packing* had been developed and cows could be turned into food quickly, easily and cheaply. But in the South, the price had dropped dramatically. The Longhorns (a breed of cattle) in Texas had been left unmanaged during the war, becoming half-wild, and their numbers had increased enormously: there were five million cows in Texas in 1865. The southern economy was badly damaged by the war and there was little demand for cows. Although a cow was worth $40 in Chicago, in Texas, it was only worth $5. In 1866, to cash in on this extra money in the North, Texans organised a large cattle drive to Sedalia, but they were prevented from crossing through Kansas by farmers worried about Texas fever.

The significance of Joseph McCoy and Abilene

In 1867, a branch line of the railroad, the Kansas Pacific, reached Abilene, Kansas. A Chicago livestock trader called Joseph McCoy realised that Abilene could be a new transit point for cattle drives. It had three key advantages.

1   Kansas had relaxed their quarantine rule in 1867, allowing Texan cattle to be driven through the state if they kept to the west of where farmers had settled. Abilene was in this westward zone.

2   There was grassland all the way from Kansas, through Indian Territory, to Texas, and there was a trade route through this grassland called the **Chisolm Trail** that cowboys could use to bring the herds north.

3   Cattle could be loaded onto railroad trucks (boxcars) at the railhead at Abilene and shipped from there to Chicago.

> ### Key term
>
> **Meat packing***
>
> Slaughtering, processing and packing of meat for distribution around the country.

Source A

Texas Longhorn cattle being loaded into a railroad boxcar in Abilene, from *Leslie's Illustrated Newspaper*, 1871.

McCoy acted quickly. He purchased 450 acres of land (at $5 per acre) and built large stockyards where cattle could be safely kept. He negotiated with the Kansas Pacific Railroad for a depot to be built on a side track where 100 railway cars could be loaded, and he constructed a hotel. He arranged for the Chisolm Trail to be marked out through Indian Territory and extended from where it ended in Wichita, Kansas, to Abilene.

Then, most importantly of all, McCoy spent $5,000 marketing his new venture. He sent riders down to Texas to tell the cattlemen there about Abilene and its facilities, promising them a safe trail up from Texas and a great opportunity for profit at the end of it. McCoy's venture was an outstanding success. 35,000 cattle were driven along the Chisholm Trail to Abilene by the end of 1867, and three million between 1867 and 1872. Abilene expanded rapidly and became famous as the first 'cow-town'. McCoy became enormously rich.

The significance of the Goodnight–Loving Trail

The **Goodnight–Loving Trail** was established in 1866 by Charles Goodnight and Oliver Loving. They realised the opportunity of selling cattle directly to new population centres in the West. Bad government planning in 1866 meant that Navajo Indians in a reservation near Fort Sumner were close to starvation. Goodnight and Loving, with 18 cowboys, drove 2,000 cattle through hostile Comanche Indian territory to reach the fort, where they were able to sell 800 cattle for around $12,000: nearly four times as much as they would have sold for in Texas.

Then, while Goodnight returned to Texas for another herd, Loving moved the remaining 1,200 cattle north and sold them to John Iliff, who had built a successful business selling beef to government workers and reservations in Colorado and Wyoming.

In 1867, Oliver Loving was injured in a Comanche attack and died of his wounds. However, Goodnight continued to drive cattle north to the booming mining towns of Colorado (700 miles from Texas). In 1868, in a deal with Iliff, Goodnight drove cattle all the way up to Cheyenne, Wyoming (near Fort Laramie), on the Union Pacific Railroad.

By 1876, Goodnight was so successful that his ranch* in Texas had expanded to one million acres. Other cattle drivers started to use the trail to Wyoming, too. As a result, Wyoming began to develop its own cattle industry (see page 83 for consequences).

Extend your knowledge

Abilene and westward expansion

1871 was Abilene's high point as a cow town: in that year, 5,000 cowboys were paid in Abilene at the end of their trails north. After 1871, Abilene began to decline in importance as other Kansas towns further west and south of Abilene got rail connections. McCoy was involved in the development of Wichita as a cow town. By the end of the 1870s, Dodge City, further west, had taken over from Wichita as the main cow town.

Key term

Ranch*
A large farm for breeding and keeping cattle, rather than for crops.

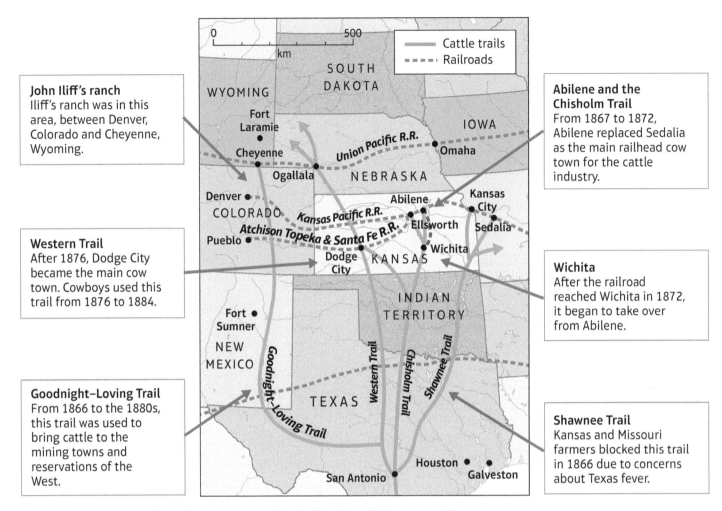

John Iliff's ranch
Iliff's ranch was in this area, between Denver, Colorado and Cheyenne, Wyoming.

Western Trail
After 1876, Dodge City became the main cow town. Cowboys used this trail from 1876 to 1884.

Goodnight–Loving Trail
From 1866 to the 1880s, this trail was used to bring cattle to the mining towns and reservations of the West.

Abilene and the Chisholm Trail
From 1867 to 1872, Abilene replaced Sedalia as the main railhead cow town for the cattle industry.

Wichita
After the railroad reached Wichita in 1872, it began to take over from Abilene.

Shawnee Trail
Kansas and Missouri farmers blocked this trail in 1866 due to concerns about Texas fever.

Figure 2.4 The main cattle trails and cow towns in the West from 1866 to the 1880s.

John Iliff and the beginnings of ranching on the Plains

In 1861, John Iliff bought a herd of cattle for $500 – a cheap price because the herd was exhausted after a long drive across the Plains and was too thin to sell for beef. Iliff had spotted an opportunity that would bring significant changes to the cattle industry.

In the same year, Colorado Territory had been created following a gold rush in the Colorado Rocky Mountains. Denver City, right at the western edge of the Plains (in the foothills of the Colorado Rockies) grew rapidly, selling supplies to gold prospectors. This meant that there was great demand for meat. However, Denver had no railroad connection (until 1870) and it was difficult and expensive to transport supplies there.

Iliff spotted the opportunity in the problem: if he could fatten his new herd up on the grass of the Plains, he would be able to sell beef for a good price to the mining towns with none of the expense and difficulty of the long drives.

In 1866, Iliff bought land for a ranch near Denver. By 1870, he had built up a huge herd on the Colorado Plains: 26,000 cattle. He had extended his original ranch to cover 16,000 acres of land northwards towards Cheyenne, using the Homestead Act to build up a patchwork of claims. He became Denver's first millionaire: selling beef to the mining towns, to the teams building the Union Pacific Railroad, and to the government for Plains Indian reservations. In 1872, he won a contract to provide beef to a reservation of 7,000 Sioux Indians.

What was most important about his success was that he had raised the majority of his herd on the Plains rather than relying only on cattle driven up from Texas. This was the start of a new phase in the cattle industry: ranching on the open range* of the Great Plains.

Source B

Extract from an obituary of 23 February 1878 in *The Denver Times* for John Iliff, 'The Cattle King of Colorado', following his death.

He went to work with a will, gave almost his entire time and generally a great share of his personal attention to his herds. He saw them grow, knew where they ranged, understood when it was a good time to buy and a good time to sell; indeed he gave his business that untiring attention that never fails to find its reward in the gains that follow. His life was a worthy example to other men, and is a fair illustration of what may be accomplished by well directed effort on the plains of the Far West.

The cattle barons

The 1870s saw a 'beef bonanza' in the West. Although the long drives from Texas continued to railheads in Kansas, the big growth was in ranching on the Plains. Through the 1870s, the cattle industry was seen as a sure way to make money: costs were low (free grass, almost free land, cheap transportation by rail) while profits were high. As a result, investors poured money into the industry.

The best way to make a lot of money was to have very large ranches and enormous herds of cattle. The consequence was that a few men, backed by rich investors, dominated the cattle industry. They were called the **cattle barons** because of their wealth and influence. In new territories, like Colorado and Wyoming, cattle barons controlled local politics as well as almost all the land. They defended their interests fiercely, especially against cattle rustling*. This would have significant consequences for law and order (see page 83).

Interpretation 1

From *The Great American Desert* (1966) by W. E. Hollon. Here he describes how the right conditions came about to cause the rapid growth of the cattle industry.

Suddenly, the right conditions fell into place… the Civil War brought an increased demand for beef… settlers learned that cattle could thrive on the native grass and survive the drastic changes in climate; the transcontinental railroads pushed to the Pacific… .

Key term

Open range*

A large area of unfenced land over which livestock roamed freely.

Exam-style question, Section A

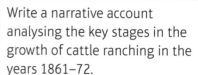

Write a narrative account analysing the key stages in the growth of cattle ranching in the years 1861–72.

You may use the following in your answer:

- Joseph McCoy and Abilene
- cattle barons

You **must** also use information of your own. **8 marks**

Exam tip

Your answer will need to consider several key stages to be effective, including at least one point that is not suggested by the question prompts, if you are to do well.

Key term

Rustling*

Stealing livestock (especially cattle).

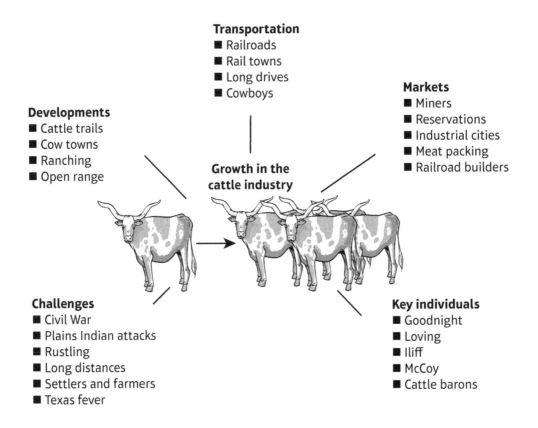

Transportation
- Railroads
- Rail towns
- Long drives
- Cowboys

Markets
- Miners
- Reservations
- Industrial cities
- Meat packing
- Railroad builders

Developments
- Cattle trails
- Cow towns
- Ranching
- Open range

Growth in the cattle industry

Challenges
- Civil War
- Plains Indian attacks
- Rustling
- Long distances
- Settlers and farmers
- Texas fever

Key individuals
- Goodnight
- Loving
- Iliff
- McCoy
- Cattle barons

Figure 2.5 Factors affecting the growth of the cattle industry before and after the Civil War.

Activity ?

Using Figure 2.5 to help you:

a explain how key individuals were able to develop new ways to meet demands for beef from different markets after the Civil War

b explain how cow towns were connected to challenges, transportation, markets and key individuals

c identify as many connections as you can between railroads and the growth in the cattle industry from 1862 to 1876.

Cowboys and changes in the cattle industry
Life on the long drive

Driving a herd of cows from Texas to Kansas up the Chisholm Trail took between two and three months. Herding cattle up the Goodnight–Loving Trail to Cheyenne could take six months. It was very challenging work because half-wild longhorn cattle were very easily scared ('spooked') into a stampede.

Stampeding cattle could get lost, injured or killed, and running for long distances meant the cows lost weight and became less valuable. The worst stampedes happened at night, when the cowboys would have to race after the cattle, trusting that their horses could see any danger. Then there were the challenges of swimming cattle across rivers, dealing with snakes and wild animals, negotiating permission to cross Indian Territory, guarding the herd from theft, and fending off attacks by Plains Indians or outlaws.

Source C

A coloured engraving from the early 1870s depicting cowboys driving cattle up the Chisolm Trail. Note the long line of cattle with cowboys spaced out along it.

Long drives often involved about 3,000 cattle, which needed around 12 cowboys to manage. Cowboys worked in outfits led by a trail boss, who was responsible for the speed the herd was moving at, and where camp would be made each night. The outfit always included a chuck wagon, which transported food, water, equipment, and a cook. There was also a wrangler, who cared for the horses: each cowboy changed horse several times a day to prevent horses getting exhausted or injured.

Outfits were hired by the owner of the herd to deliver his cattle in good condition by an agreed time. In the 1870s, trail bosses were paid around $100 a month for the Chisolm Trail, while the rest of the outfit each got between $25 and $30.

Cowboys on the trail slept in the open, taking it in turns to stay awake and guard the herd through the night. When the cattle woke up, they were allowed to graze for a while in preparation for the day's travel, and then organised into a long line, with cowboys at the front, along the sides and at the rear. At the end of the day, having travelled around 15 or 20 miles, the cowboys would herd the cattle together so it was easier to guard.

Extend your knowledge

Crossing Indian Territory

The Chisholm Trail went through Indian Territory, the land (now Oklahoma) that had been granted to the eastern tribes of American Indians moved west by the Indian Removal Act (see page 16). These tribes required payment from the cowboys in return for permission to cross their lands. Warriors patrolled the lands to make sure payments were collected. Conflicts sometimes occurred when trail bosses refused to pay.

At the end of the trail, in a cow town like Abilene, the cowboys would herd the cattle into the stockyards for buyers to inspect. Once the cattle were were sold, the cowboys would move the cattle into the railroad boxcars. Then the outfit was paid. (This process is shown in Source A on page 50.)

Once they had been paid, cowboys would get cleaned up, purchase the fanciest new clothes they could afford, and proceed to get drunk, go dancing with the town's available female population, gamble and fight. Cowboys often spent all their money in town and would then have to borrow money to get back to Texas to find work until the next trail the following spring.

Life on the ranch

Cattle in Texas were raised on ranches, which often covered huge areas of open land. Through the winter, the cattle roamed freely, mixing together with cattle from other ranches. During the winter months, most ranches did not employ many cowboys. Cowboys either got a different job, such as working in a bar, or rode from ranch to ranch hoping to earn some money. Cowboys who were kept on over the winter spent their time repairing equipment, riding out to see if any animals had got into difficulty, and planning the year ahead.

The real ranch work began in early spring with the round-up. This often involved cowboys from several ranches all working together, under the command of the round-up boss. Teams of cowboys fanned out from a central location on the range, then gradually worked their way back in, driving ahead of them all the cattle they had found. Some cattle took a lot of finding, hiding in dense bushes or at the bottom of gullies, sometimes getting themselves stuck in marshes or quicksand. When all the cattle were rounded up, cowboys began the work of separating them out according to ownership. Cattle were branded to show which ranch they belonged to, and in the spring new calves would also have to be branded with the same mark as its mother.

Source D

A 19th-century engraving of a round-up. It was unusual for older men to work as cowboys because it was such a tough, demanding way of life.

Life on the ranch was hard work: usually too hard for anyone much older than their early 20s. Older cowboys either found new jobs in towns, or set up ranches of their own. Ranch-hands on small ranches would live with the rancher and his family, but on most ranches there was a bunkhouse where all the cowboys lived together. The bunkhouse was more comfortable than living outdoors on a long trail, but they were usually cold and draughty during the winter. There was not much entertainment and often there were strict rules, for example, Charles Goodnight banned gambling on his ranches. Once or twice a year there were dances at local towns, which was the highpoint of the ranch's social life.

Changes on the Plains

Ranches on the Plains were open range and they carried out spring round-ups in just the same way as in Texas. Although the Plains ranches in the 1870s were much closer to railheads than Texas ranches in the 1860s, cowboys still needed to drive the herds over the Plains from the ranch to the railhead: but now the job took days rather than months.

A significant difference was winter on the Plains. Heavy snow brought new problems. If snow and ice was too deep, the cattle could not get to the grass underneath, or could not break through ice to get water. Cowboys would have to ride out during blizzards to find the herds, make paths for them to get out of snowdrifts, break the ice at waterholes for them to drink, and find sheltered spots where they could stay out of the wind. On the biggest ranches, cowboys would be sent out over the winter to stay in sod houses or cabins dotted round the perimeter of the ranch. Sometimes these cowboys spent the winter on their own: a cold and lonely way of life.

Activities ?

1 Compare the life of cowboys who went on long drives with the lives of cowboys who lived on ranches. Identify at least one similarity and one difference.
2 Write a letter home from a teenage cowboy who has just completed his first spring round-up. Describe the challenges of the job and what the cowboy enjoyed and did not enjoy.
3 John Iliff introduced the idea of ranching on the Plains. Describe three ways in which ranching on the Plains meant changes in the life of cowboys.

Rivalry between ranchers and homesteaders

Ranching on the open range needed a lot of land – at least 2,000 acres and preferably much more. The ranchers did not buy all this land: that would have been a lot of money for even the richest ranchers. Instead, they made use of public land. Federal law said that everyone was able to pasture livestock on public land. This worked fine when there was no competition for the land. Ranchers divided up the range between themselves.

The Homestead Act allowed people to file claims up to 160-acre chunks of public land. When homesteading spread to ranching country, it threatened ranching. Ranchers used many different tactics to block homesteading on 'their' public land.

- They would file claims under the Homestead Act themselves for the bits of land on the ranch that contained waterholes or springs. This made the rest of the public land on the ranch unattractive to potential settlers as there would be no access to water.
- Ranch-hands and family members would file Homestead Act claims to parcels of land throughout the ranch area and then hand those rights over to the ranch owner.
- Ranches involving railroad land bought a lot of land from the railroad companies (if they had the money). This land was mixed together with public land, in a design like a chessboard. By fencing off the ranch's sections, the ranchers could make it impossible for anyone else to access the public land mixed up with it.
- Rich ranchers took homesteaders to court over claims, knowing that most homesteaders did not have the money to pay lawyers and court costs and so would have to give up their claims.
- Some ranchers also threatened homesteaders with violence, damaged their crops and accused them of rustling cows from the ranch's herd: stealing a cow carried severe punishments in all the 'cattle states', whose economies depended on the cattle industry.

Ranchers

Ranching relied on access to huge amounts of **public** grazing land.

Ranchers used legal and illegal tactics to block homesteaders from claiming public land that ranching relied on.

v.

Homesteaders

Homesteading turned small parcels of public land into **private** farms.

Homesteaders were accused of cattle rustling – stealing the free-roaming cattle of the ranchers. Ranchers also complained that homesteaders' barbed wire fences harmed their animals.

Figure 2.6 The rivalry between ranchers and homesteaders.

There were often problems when cows strayed onto fields and ate crops. The ranchers said that cows had a legal right to roam on the range and farmers were to blame if they had not fenced their land, or if the fences were not strong enough to keep the cattle back. Farmers said the ranchers were to blame if they had not fenced off their property to prevent their cattle from straying.

While state governments wrestled with laws over responsibility, disputes between ranchers and homesteaders added to the strain on local law enforcement. Long-running tensions sometimes developed into open conflicts between ranchers and homesteaders, known as range wars. The most famous range war, the Johnson County War, is covered in Chapter 3 (page 83).

Conflicts over sheep farming

There were also conflicts between cattlemen and sheepherders, both of whom were competing for the use of public lands for grazing. Cattle ranchers claimed that sheep ate grass down to the roots, leaving nothing for cows, and that sheep spread disease: sheep scab.

Large-scale sheep farming started in the 1870s in the West, in places where cattle herding was already established, including Texas and Wyoming. When cattle ranchers began fencing off grazing land to stop other livestock using it, sheepherders would cut the fences. Cattle barons in these areas dominated local government, which meant that cattle ranchers tended to win all the court cases, including over fence cutting. Violent clashes between cattle ranchers and sheepherders resulted in several deaths in the 1870s.

Exam-style question, Section A

Explain **two** consequences of the development of ranching on the Plains in the years 1866–76. **8 marks**

Exam tip

Remember to include **two** consequences in your answer and spend equal time on both.

Summary

- The period from 1862 to 1876 saw rapid growth of the cattle industry, including the development of ranching on the Great Plains.
- Goodnight, Iliff and McCoy pioneered new ways to meet growing demand for beef in both eastern and western USA, all of which had important consequences for the cattle industry.
- Cowboys on long drives had very different lives from when they worked on ranches. There were both freedoms and dangers on the long drive.
- As homesteaders began to claim the public land the ranchers depended on, the two groups began to clash.

Checkpoint

Strengthen

S1 Explain why the town of Abilene is significant in the development of the cattle industry.

S2 Describe the ways in which McCoy, Goodnight and Iliff changed the cattle industry.

S3 Why did the use of public land become a cause of conflict between ranchers and homesteaders?

Challenge

C1 Explain how the development of railroads across the West influenced the growth of the cattle industry.

C2 What impacts do you predict that the spread of ranching across the West had on the Plains Indians' way of life?

How confident do you feel about your answers to these questions? Figure 2.5 (page 54) groups together some of the key factors and events in the growth of the cattle industry in this period and could help you to think through the ways these key factors and events linked up.

2.3 Changes in the way of life of the Plains Indians

Learning outcomes

- Understand how changes affected the life of Plains Indians.
- Understand the US government policy towards Plains Indians and the impact of this.

The expansion of the railroad, the growing cattle industry and gold prospecting all increased the pressures on the Plains Indians' traditional way of life. The resources they depended on were shrinking as white America expanded.

The impact of railroads

Under the Fort Laramie Treaty (1851), tribes were to allow railroad surveyors and construction teams to enter their lands. However, Plains Indians were unaware of the huge land grants that financed the railroad and the impact of the railroads on buffalo hunting. Land grants took land away from the tribes and reduced grazing for buffalo; while settlers meant fences were built, which blocked buffalo movements and disrupted hunts. Railroads were also required to fence off tracks running through settled lands. Most significantly, as shown in the next chapter (page 90), railroads enabled the extermination of the buffalo by hunters.

As part of the Pacific Railroad Act, the government began to 'extinguish' any Plains Indian rights to land along the railroad routes. The route of the Union Pacific Railroad went through Pawnee lands. The Pawnee were friendly to the US government because they needed its support against enemy northern Plains Indian tribes. In 1870, the Pawnee agreed to move to a reservation in Indian Territory. Other tribes in the way of the railroad, such as the Omaha, Santee Sioux and Winnebago tribes, also signed treaties to live on reservations in Nebraska.

The route of the Northern Pacific Railroad, however, ran through Dakota, Montana and Washington territories where tens of thousands of Plains Indians still lived traditional lives that depended on buffalo hunting. Construction began in 1870. The railroad was given 40 million acres of land grants to sell to settlers. This railroad triggered conflicts that grew into the Great Sioux War (Chapter 3).

Source A

An 1868 engraving of Plains Indians attacking a train along the Union Pacific Railroad.

The cattle industry

Cattle and buffalo had the same diet: grass. Consequently, as cattle numbers increased on the Plains, buffalo numbers declined.

- In 1860, there were 130,000 cattle in the West, all in Kansas and Nebraska.
- In 1880, there were 4.5 million cattle: half of those in Colorado, Wyoming, Montana and Dakota.

As buffalo became hard to find, some Plains Indians went to work as cowboys while others worked on ranches, especially in Indian Territory. Ranching or working on a white man's ranch was much more of a settled way of life, which took Plains Indians away from traditional lifestyles. It meant they worked for money and depended on ranchers for employment.

Activities ?

1   Identify three pressures on the Plains Indians that increased tensions between tribes and white Americans. Explain how each of these pressures led to increased tensions.

2   Produce a similar diagram to Figure 2.7 of your own (you could use photos or your own drawings). Expand the captions for each picture to explain, in your own words, why they led to increased tension or how they resulted from conflict between white Americans and Plains Indians.

The cattle trails also had an impact on Plains Indian ways of life (see page 55) and Plains Indians organised patrols to monitor who was using the trails. Other tribes, especially the Comanche, resented any trespassers on their lands, and attacked cowboys and stole horses and cattle from long drives. This resulted in protection from the US Army, who would sometimes ride out to attack the tribes, making things worse.

Gold prospecting

In California, gold prospectors had murdered American Indians as well as forcibly removing tribes to get them away from possible claims to gold. Also, the influx of men from all over the world brought new diseases that devastated American Indian populations. New towns developed, with churches, schools and stores, which were all alien to American Indian culture. Of all the threats to American Indian ways of life, gold prospecting was the most catastrophic because the changes it brought happened so rapidly.

Any hint of gold brought thousands of prospectors to an area, regardless of any treaties. In 1862, gold was discovered in Montana Territory. The quickest route from the East to the mining area was through the Lakota Sioux's hunting grounds. Thousands travelled along this route, called the **Bozeman Trail**, despite this being against the terms of the Fort Laramie Treaty. Red Cloud's War (see page 65) was a direct consequence of these tensions.

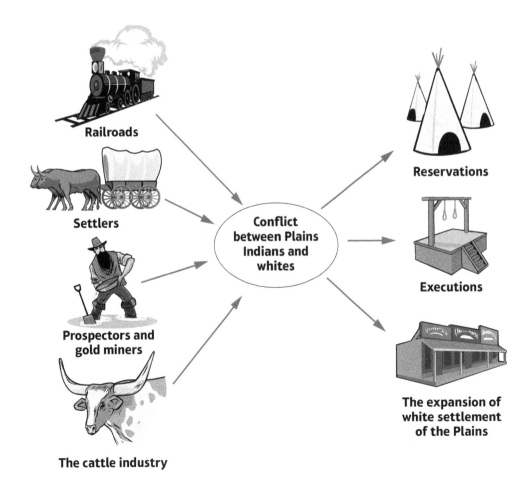

Railroads

Settlers

Prospectors and gold miners

The cattle industry

Conflict between Plains Indians and whites

Reservations

Executions

The expansion of white settlement of the Plains

Figure 2.7 Pressures on the Plains Indians after 1862 and their consequences.

US government policy towards Plains Indians and its impacts

As more white Americans moved onto the Plains the government continued its policy of moving Plains Indians onto reservations. In return, the US government guaranteed that the Plains Indians would:

- not lose any more land
- be protected from attack by whites
- be given yearly payments (in money but also in food, livestock, clothing and farming equipment).

Why did Plains Indians move to reservations?

Often Plains Indian tribes agreed to move to reservations, or agreed to a reduction of their lands into a reservation, because their council felt there was no other way for the tribe to survive. White expansion and dwindling food supplies forced them to make this decision. The US government made promises to chiefs that the tribes would be well cared for on the reservation, with regular supplies of food and the opportunity to continue hunting on hunting grounds. However, once it became clear that the government rarely carried out these promises, other tribes resisted reservations: either by refusing to move to them, or not staying on them. The US Army was used to force Plains Indians to move to reservations or return to them if they left.

Impacts of the reservations

The government's belief was that reservations would benefit Plains Indians. They could learn about farming and Christianity, and their children could be taught to read and write. They could also learn about white American values. The US Army would ensure that no warrior bands from other tribes or outlaws would raid the reservation (and also stop warrior bands from the reservation doing any raiding of their own). However, there were major problems with reservations that had serious and negative impacts on Plains Indian people.

- The reservations showed no understanding of Plains Indian cultural values. Treaties about reservations were agreed with chiefs, but chiefs often had no authority to make bands or brotherhoods stay on the reservation. Reservations were sometimes a long way from the tribe's sacred places and traditional enemies were sometimes placed on the same reservation (e.g. Apache and Navajo).

American Indian homelands and reservations 1862

American Indian homelands and reservations 1876

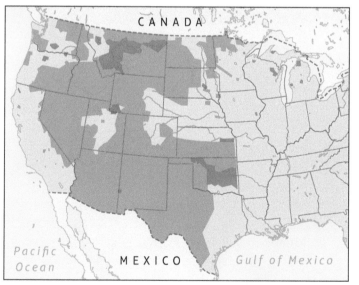

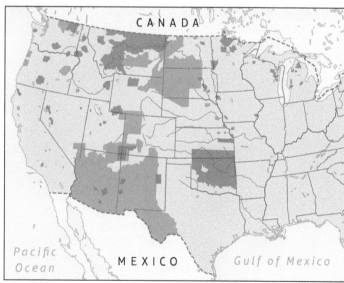

Figure 2.8 Changes in American Indian lands between 1862 and 1876. The blue areas are homelands where American Indians continued to live freely. The red areas are reservations.

- The challenges of farming on the Plains were even worse for Plains Indians than for white settlers because reservations often had very poor farming land (that whites did not want) and some tribes had no traditions of farming at all. When crops failed the Plains Indians had to be supplied with food by the government.

- The management of reservations was the responsibility of the Bureau of Indian Affairs. It appointed agents who ran each reservation from an Agency located on the reservation. These men were often corrupt and cheated the tribes in order to make themselves wealthy.

- White settlers were angry at the size of some reservations and complained that the Plains Indians were being treated better than they were. The government used any excuse to reduce the size of reservations, breaking treaties by doing so, and making it ever harder for the tribes to survive.

President Grant's 'Peace Policy' (1868)

Problems on the reservations led directly to conflicts between desperate Plains Indians and the US Army. In 1868, President Ulysses S. Grant put forward a '**Peace Policy**.' This aimed to calm tensions by improving the management of the reservation system.

Source B

From President Grant's State of the Union speech, 6 December 1869.

```
The building of railroads, and the access
thereby given to all the agricultural and
mineral regions of the country, is rapidly
bringing civilized settlements into contact
with all the tribes of Indians. No matter
what ought to be the relations between such
settlements and the [Indians], the fact is
they do not harmonize well, and one or the
other has to give way in the end. A system
which looks to the extinction of a race
is too horrible for a nation to adopt...
I see no substitute for such a system,
except in placing all the Indians on large
reservations, as rapidly as it can be done,
and giving them absolute protection there.
```

The main change in the policy was to replace corrupt reservation agents with religious men, specifically Quakers who had a strong reputation for fairness, justice and peacefulness. Grant also appointed an American Indian, Ely Parker, as the Commissioner of Indian Affairs. The US government put forward a budget of $2 million to ensure that Plains Indians already living on reservations were properly cared for, and to set up reservations for tribes currently roaming free. Plains Indians who refused to go to the reservations were to be treated as hostile and would be attacked by the army.

Ely Parker pushed for a further change in government policy. Instead of negotiating treaties with tribes, he argued that Plains Indians should be treated as 'helpless and ignorant wards' (a ward is a child that is put under the protection of an adult guardian). The government should decide what was best for its Plains Indian 'wards', make sure they obeyed and then treat them fairly.

Source C

This engraving of Ely S. Parker was made in 1866.

These views came into law in the Indian Appropriation Act of 1871. This act declared that Plains Indian nations or tribes would no longer be recognised 'as an independent nation, tribe, or power with whom the United States may contract by treaty'. While previously-agreed treaties still applied, this Act did make it easier for the US government to take land (not under treaty) from Plains Indians and give it to settlers.

Activities ?

1 Name three differences between life on the Plains Indian homelands and life on a reservation.

2 Look at Source B. Explain the consequences of Grant's view of the Plains Indians.

3 Working with a partner, describe the changes in government policy towards the Plains Indians from 1834 to 1871.

Conflict with the Plains Indians

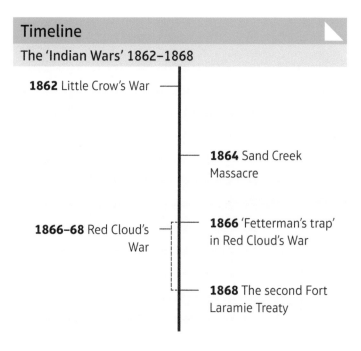

Timeline

The 'Indian Wars' 1862–1868

1862 Little Crow's War

1864 Sand Creek Massacre

1866–68 Red Cloud's War

1866 'Fetterman's trap' in Red Cloud's War

1868 The second Fort Laramie Treaty

Little Crow's War (1862)

Little Crow was a chief of a band of the Dakota Sioux from an area in Minnesota. In 1850, there were 50,000 Plains Indians in Minnesota and only 6,000 whites. However, the numbers of white settlers were rapidly increasing, and the numbers of animals to hunt was rapidly declining.

In 1851, Dakota Sioux bands, including Little Crow's band, signed a treaty and agreed to move to two reservations. They gave up 24 million acres of their land in return for a payment of $1.4 million with an annuity (yearly payment) of $80,000: some in cash and some as provisions. Although the reservations were both small, Little Crow thought that the money would buy security for his people while they adapted to new ways of life.

There were immediate problems with the treaty.

- In the years before the treaty, the Dakota Sioux had built up debts with traders. The treaty included a clause that stated that before the Dakota Sioux got any of their money, they would have to pay back $200,000 to the traders. They refused to do this, giving the government an excuse not to pay the $1.4 million and to delay paying annuities for months.

- It soon became clear that the reservations could not produce enough food for the Dakota Sioux to survive on over winter. When bands left the reservation to hunt, the reservation agent refused to let them have any supplies from their annuity in punishment.

- The Agency and local traders cheated the Dakota Sioux. The Agency would hold onto annuity payments for several weeks until the starving Dakota Sioux agreed to very high prices for food. The Agency also brought provisions that were often inedible. In this way, almost all of the tribe's annuity would be taken as soon as it arrived from the government.

- Settlers began to take other pieces of reservation land along the Minnesota River that were good for farming.

- Trouble repeatedly flared up as warrior brotherhoods launched raids to capture resources, or broke into the Agency storehouses to steal provisions.

In 1858, the Dakota Sioux were made to sign away half of the reservation in return for money to pay the traders' debts. Little Crow said 'you promised us that we should have this same land forever, and yet now you want to take half of it away'.

By August 1862, the Dakota Sioux were in a desperate situation. Crops had failed and late payments from the government meant they had no money to buy food. People tried to survive by eating grass. The reservation agent showed no sympathy, even though his storehouse was full of provisions, and local traders refused to let the Dakota Sioux buy food on credit.

The Civil War meant the US Army was fighting the Confederates. So, Little Crow and other chiefs believed the time was right to take back what they felt was rightfully theirs. They took food and provisions from the Agency's warehouses and distributed it amongst their starving people before burning down the Agency buildings. They then attacked the settlers' towns and army forts. Unfortunately, many young warriors had little respect for the chiefs who had signed away their lands. Little Crow did not think it was right to kill those who were no threat, but the warriors slaughtered settlers, including women and children. In all, around 600 settlers and US soldiers were killed.

As more troops arrived, Little Crow and his followers fled into Dakota. White Minnesotans were determined that the hostile Dakota Sioux must be punished. 400 Dakota Sioux warriors were put on trial, and most were sentenced to death without any evidence of their guilt. President Lincoln insisted that only those proven to be guilty of murder or rape should be executed – 38 men.

The rest of the Dakota Sioux in Minnesota were moved to the Crow Creek Reservation: isolated, dry lands in south Dakota, in which many starved to death in their first winter (1863–64), or to other reservations in Nebraska. Bounties (reward money) were paid for the scalps of any Dakota Sioux found hiding in Minnesota.

Little Crow himself had managed to make it back into Minnesota with his son, but a hunter saw him and shot him. The hunter cut off Little Crow's scalp for the bounty, and another man later chopped off his head.

Activities ?

1 A director is planning a short film about Little Crow's War and wants a list of the main scenes. Identify the key events in the story to help her with her planning.

2 Identify points from the account of Little Crow's War that could be used as examples to support the following statements:

   a The 'Peace Policy' of 1868 aimed to put right the mismanagement of some reservations.

   b White settlers viewed Plains Indians as sub-human vermin that needed to be exterminated.

   c Plains Indian chiefs were not leaders of their tribe in the way that white Americans assumed.

The Sand Creek Massacre (1864)

The Fort Laramie Treaty of 1851 guaranteed the Cheyenne and Arapaho large amounts of land (see the map on page 29). However, when gold was discovered in Colorado Territory in 1858, prospectors began crossing over Cheyenne and Arapaho land, using up the grass and scaring away buffalo and deer. Some of them began settling and demanded that the US government move the Plains Indians onto reservations.

In the **Treaty of Fort Wise** (1861), Arapaho and Cheyenne chiefs (including Black Kettle) agreed to move to a reservation in east Colorado. But many young warriors, in brotherhoods knowns as the Dog Soldiers, rejected the treaty – they had not signed it – and remained on their old lands. There were frequent conflicts between the Dog Soldiers and prospectors crossing Colorado Territory.

After three years of raids and attacks, Black Kettle, government officials and army commanders tried to reach an agreement. Believing he was under army protection, Black Kettle set up camp at Sand Creek. However, the Territory's governor, John Evans, was determined to 'kill and destroy' hostile Plains Indians. He appointed Colonel Chivington, a Civil War hero, to do the job.

On 29 November 1864, Chivington led 700 cavalry troops on a dawn raid on Black Kettle's camp. Chivington claimed his troops fought a tremendous battle against 1,000 warriors. This was not true. The camp put up a white flag of surrender, but Chivington and his men still massacred over 130 men, women, children and babies. They scalped their victims and took other body parts as trophies, which were displayed in local saloons.

Source D

An engraving of the Sand Creek Massacre. This is a colour version of the original engraving, which was made in 1868.

Black Kettle escaped and carried news of the massacre to other tribes. The Dog Soldiers felt they had been right all along: the massacre at Sand Creek showed the white Americans should never be trusted and must be fought. They attacked forts and killed many white settlers across Colorado Territory.

The government was under great pressure in the Civil War and could not afford to send thousands of troops to Colorado to fight Plains Indians, so a new treaty was agreed in 1865. The Cheyenne and Arapaho would move to a large reservation south of the Arkansas River, and generous payments would be made to survivors of the Sand Creek Massacre.

However, once the Civil War was won, the US government backed out of the deal. Instead, in a treaty made in 1867, the Cheyenne and Arapaho were moved to a reservation half the size of what they had been promised in 1865. They were allowed to hunt buffalo in their old hunting grounds, but only as long as the buffalo remained. They also had to stay away from white people's property. No compensation was paid to the survivors of the Sand Creek Massacre. Black Kettle himself died in 1868, in another massacre of Plains Indians by US troops.

Red Cloud's War (1866–68)

Red Cloud was a respected war chief and warrior of the Lakota Sioux. Like Little Crow and Black Kettle, he saw his way of life coming under threat from whites.

When gold was discovered in Montana in 1862, prospectors from the East began to use a short cut off the Oregon Trail known as the Bozeman Trail, which crossed important Lakota Sioux hunting grounds. By 1865, 2,000 people had travelled the Bozeman Trail, despite numerous attacks by angry Lakota Sioux.

The Bozeman Trail broke the Fort Laramie Treaty of 1851. In 1866, the government called a council to discuss a new treaty. Red Cloud was invited together with other Lakota Sioux chiefs. The government aimed to get the Lakota Sioux to allow people to travel safely along the Bozeman Trail in return for gifts and a promise that their hunting lands would not be disturbed.

Just before the council began, Red Cloud discovered that the army had already brought materials to build forts along the Bozeman Trail. He realised that the government was only trying to get the Lakota Sioux to agree to something that was going to happen anyway. He knew what had happened to Little Crow and did not trust the US government. Red Cloud believed the Lakota Sioux were forced to choose between fighting and starvation. He chose to fight.

Not all the Lakota Sioux agreed with him, especially those that hunted in lands away from the Bozeman Trail. Others believed that it was useless to fight the whites, and better to sign the treaty and get what they could from the government.

However, many other bands did follow Red Cloud in a two-year fight to prevent the Bozeman Trail from being used. They attacked soldiers and other workers building the forts. Red Cloud was joined by two other determined Lakota Sioux leaders, Sitting Bull and Crazy Horse (see page 10), and was able to bring Cheyenne and Arapaho bands to join his war. In total, Red Cloud's War may have involved nearly 3,000 Plains Indian warriors, fighting around 700 US soldiers.

Source E

A photograph (from 1891) showing Chief Red Cloud on the right of the picture, with another Lakota Sioux chief called American Horse, who is dressed in western clothing.

In December 1866, there was an attack on men sent out to cut wood at one of the new forts. Captain William Fetterman led a group of 80 cavalrymen to protect them. The Lakota Sioux had developed a tactic of sending out a couple of scouts who deliberately got spotted by US cavalry, then galloped off leading the pursuing cavalry into an ambush. Even though this was a well-known tactic of the Lakota Sioux, Captain Fetterman fell for it. He and all his men were killed by a much larger force in what became known as **Fetterman's Trap**

The Lakota Sioux surrounded Fort Phil Kearny, one of the forts on the Bozeman Trail. Troops could not leave the fort and no traveller could move along the Bozeman Trail. The Lakota Sioux victory at Fort Phil Kearny was proof for the government that old approaches were not working. A Peace Commission reported in 1867 that the best way to end the conflict was to convince Plains Indians to give up their lands and move to reservations further west.

The second Fort Laramie Treaty (1868)

As a consequence of Red Cloud's success, the US government agreed to close the Bozeman Trail (another route to the gold fields had already been found). In return, Red Cloud agreed to take his people to a reservation in Dakota. The second Fort Laramie Treaty recognised that this Great Sioux Reservation was to be for the exclusive use of the Sioux nation. Not all of those who had fought with Red Cloud agreed with his signing the Treaty. Chief Sitting Bull and Crazy Horse were amongst those who refused to sign.

Source F

An extract from the 1868 Fort Laramie Treaty

The United States hereby agrees... that the country north of the North Platte river and east of the summits of the Big Horn mountains shall be held and considered to be... Indian territory, and also... that no white person or persons shall be permitted to settle upon or occupy any portion of [that land]; or without the consent of the Indians... to pass through [that land]; and it is further agreed by the United States, that within ninety days after the conclusion of peace with all the bands of the Sioux nation, the military posts now established in the territory... shall be abandoned, and that the road [the Bozeman Trail] leading to them and by them to the settlements in the Territory of Montana shall be closed.

Activity ?

Why was Red Cloud able to achieve a victory for his people, while Black Kettle and Little Crow were not? Discuss this question as a class or in groups.

Summary

- White invasion of Plains Indian lands put enormous pressures on the Plains Indians.
- Corrupt management of reservation food supplies caused desperation and then conflict.
- Government policy remained focused on moving Plains Indians to reservations.

Checkpoint

Strengthen

S1 Which tribes did Little Crow, Black Kettle and Red Cloud lead?

S2 Describe three causes of conflict between Plains Indians and white Americans.

Challenge

C1 Thinking ahead, what consequences do you predict for President Grant's 'Peace Policy'? Do you expect it to be broadly successful, with Plains Indians managing to integrate into white American society? If not, why not?

How confident do you feel about your answers to these questions? Figure 2.7 (page 60) models a way of representing factors and consequences of key events as a diagram. Try this approach for different topics.

Recap: Development of the Plains, c1862–c1876

Recall quiz

1 In what year did the American Civil War end – and who won?

2 How many acres were allotted to someone making a claim under the Homestead Act?

3 What were the names of the two companies set up by the Pacific Railroad Act?

4 In what year was the First Transcontinental Railroad completed?

5 What was invented in 1874 that made it much easier and cheaper for homesteaders to protect their crops and livestock?

6 What was the name of the trail that was used to drive cattle from Texas to Abilene?

7 Who pioneered the first ranch on the Great Plains?

8 Describe one way in which cattle ranchers tried to block homesteaders from settling on the public land used by their ranches.

9 What was the name of the trail that triggered Red Cloud's War?

10 Which US President introduced his 'Peace Policy' in 1868?

Activities

1 Create three large timelines like the ones below. Decide which of the key events provided belongs to which timeline(s) and add them to the correct year on your timelines. The same event can appear on more than one timeline.

2 Which one event do you think was the most significant for the settlement of the American West in the period from 1862 to 1876? Explain the choice you have made.

Exam-style question, Section A

Write a narrative account analysing the events of the Indian Wars, 1862–1868.

You may use the following in your answer:

• Little Crow's War (1862)

• The second Fort Laramie Treaty (1868)

You **must** also use information of your own.   **8 marks**

Exam tip

Include key events and make links between them to give an explained account. Make sure that you only cover the years given in the question and remember to add at least one of your own points.

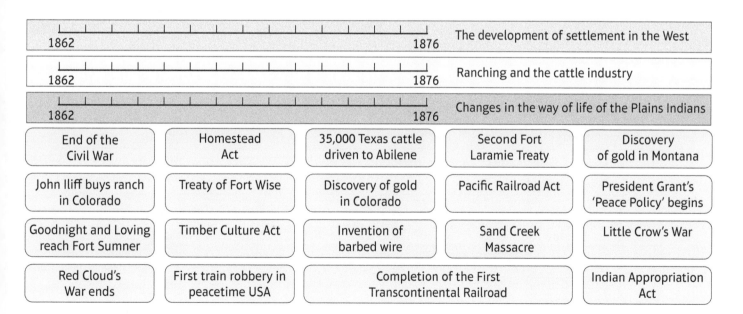

| | The development of settlement in the West |
| 1862 ... 1876 | |

| | Ranching and the cattle industry |
| 1862 ... 1876 | |

| | Changes in the way of life of the Plains Indians |
| 1862 ... 1876 | |

End of the Civil War	Homestead Act	35,000 Texas cattle driven to Abilene	Second Fort Laramie Treaty	Discovery of gold in Montana
John Iliff buys ranch in Colorado	Treaty of Fort Wise	Discovery of gold in Colorado	Pacific Railroad Act	President Grant's 'Peace Policy' begins
Goodnight and Loving reach Fort Sumner	Timber Culture Act	Invention of barbed wire	Sand Creek Massacre	Little Crow's War
Red Cloud's War ends	First train robbery in peacetime USA	Completion of the First Transcontinental Railroad		Indian Appropriation Act

Writing historically: linking information

When you explain events and their consequences, you need to show how your ideas link together.

Learning outcomes

By the end of this lesson, you will understand how to:

- use present participles to link ideas clearly and concisely
- use other non-finite clauses to link ideas clearly and concisely.

Definitions

Non-finite clause: a clause beginning with a non-finite verb. These can be any of the below.

A present participle: a verb form ending in *-ing*, e.g. 'running', 'building', 'forming', 'falling', etc.

A past participle: a verb form often ending in *-ed*, e.g. 'formed', 'happened', etc, although there are several exceptions, e.g. 'ran', 'built', 'fell', etc.

An infinitive: the 'root' verb form, which often begins with 'to', e.g. 'to run', 'to build', 'to form'.

How can I link ideas using present participles?

You can structure sentences to link related ideas in a number of different ways. One way is to use a **present participle** to create a **non-finite clause**.

For example, look at all the different ways in which two sentences in the example answer below can be linked to this exam-style question:

> Explain **two** consequences of the opening of the First Transcontinental Railroad (1869). **(8 marks)**

| With the opening of the railroad, homesteaders could solve some of the key problems in farming. | + | It enabled them to transport goods manufactured in the East more quickly and in bulk. | = |

> With the opening of the railroad, homesteaders could solve some of the key problems in farming, enabling them to transport goods manufactured in the East more quickly and in bulk.

This present participle clearly and succinctly links the two points together.

1. Look at the sentences below. How could you link them using a present participle?

| The railroad allowed homesteaders to bring in machinery, such as wind pumps. | + | This made farming much more efficient. | =? |

| The railroad meant that it was much easier for people to make the journey from the East to the West over land. | + | This made it much safer, quicker and easier. | =? |

2. a. Choose **either** of the pairs of sentences above. How else could you link them? Experiment with two or three different ways.

b. Which of your experiments expresses the information most clearly? Write a sentence explaining your choice.

How can I link ideas using other kinds of non-finite verbs?

There are three forms of non-finite verb:

- **Infinitives** (e.g. 'to open', 'to make', 'to mean')
- **Present participles** (e.g. 'opening', 'making', 'meaning')
- **Past participles** (e.g. 'opened', 'made', 'meant')

Compare the sentences below, written in response to the exam-style question on the previous page:

> The First Transcontinental Railroad was opened in 1869. The railroad made a significant difference to the efficiency and productivity of farmers in the West.

This non-finite clause allows the writer to connect these two points much more neatly.

> Opened in 1869, the First Transcontinental Railroad made a significant difference to the efficiency and productivity of farmers in the West.

Now compare these sentences, also written in response to the exam-style question on the previous page:

> Homesteaders could bring in barbed wire. This meant they could fence off and protect crops from cattle.

This non-finite verb allows the writer to connect these two points much more neatly.

> Homesteaders could bring in barbed wire to fence off and protect crops from cattle.

3. How many of these points can you link using non-finite verbs?

> Homesteaders could bring in wind pumps.
> These helped with irrigating the land.
> This made the land more fertile.

Did you notice?

Non-finite clauses can often be positioned at different points in a sentence without affecting its meaning. Experiment with one or two of the sentences above, trying the non-finite clause in different positions.

Improving an answer

4. Look at the points noted below in response to this exam-style question:

> Explain the importance of cattle trails for the development of the cattle industry in the 1860s. **(8 marks)**

> Cattle trails were very important to the cattle industry.
> Cowboys herded large herds of cattle from Texas to the railheads in Kansas and Missouri.
> Animals worth $5 in Texas could be sold for $40 in Chicago.
> Cattle were loaded onto railroad boxcars at railheads.
> The trails helped make some people very rich.

a. Experiment with different ways of linking some or all of the points using non-finite verbs.

b. Look carefully at all of the sentences you have written. Which ones work well, clearly and briefly linking ideas? Which do not? Use your findings to write a final redraft of the notes above, aiming to make your sentences as clear and concise as possible.

03 | Conflicts and conquest, c1876–c1895

1876 saw a disastrous defeat for the US Army by the Plains Indians, which radically changed government attitudes. By 1877, Sioux resistance was all but over, but army harassment of Plains Indians continued until the Wounded Knee Massacre in 1890.

Farming on the Plains had made great progress due to technological developments and improvements in farming methods. This gave a big 'push' to settlement, which put more pressure on the government to release more reservation land for white Americans to homestead. The cattle industry enjoyed its 'beef bonanza' during the 1870s and early 1880s, with huge profits being made by the cattle barons of the open range.

The good years on the Plains came to a devastating end in the winter of 1886–87, however, revealing that open ranching was unsustainable. This meant changes for the lives of cowboys, and intensified conflicts between big ranchers and homesteaders. This caused more problems for law and order, as the range wars over land-use dragged in gunslingers like Billy the Kid and Wyatt Earp.

For the Plains Indians, 1876 marked the end of government toleration of separate American Indian nations within the USA. Reservations were cut down to scraps of territory and several methods were used to destroy Plains Indian identities, so Plains Indians would stop resisting the spread of 'civilisation' and surrender to the American way of life.

Learning outcomes

By the end of this chapter, you will:

- understand how changes in farming, the cattle industry and settlement affected the development of the West
- understand the ways in which conflict and tension in the West increased because of different ideas about how the land should be used
- understand how government policies for dealing with the Plains Indians led to the destruction of their way of life.

3.1 Changes in farming, the cattle industry and settlement

Learning outcomes

- Understand the impact of new technology and new farming methods.
- Understand changes in the cattle industry following the winter of 1886–87.
- Investigate the continued growth of settlement through the Exoduster movement and the Oklahoma Land Rush.

Changes in farming

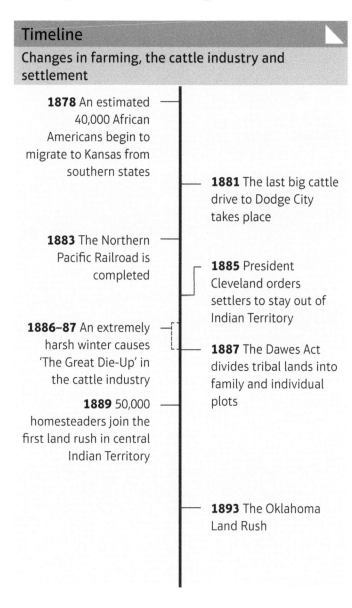

Timeline

Changes in farming, the cattle industry and settlement

1878 An estimated 40,000 African Americans begin to migrate to Kansas from southern states

1881 The last big cattle drive to Dodge City takes place

1883 The Northern Pacific Railroad is completed

1885 President Cleveland orders settlers to stay out of Indian Territory

1886–87 An extremely harsh winter causes 'The Great Die-Up' in the cattle industry

1887 The Dawes Act divides tribal lands into family and individual plots

1889 50,000 homesteaders join the first land rush in central Indian Territory

1893 The Oklahoma Land Rush

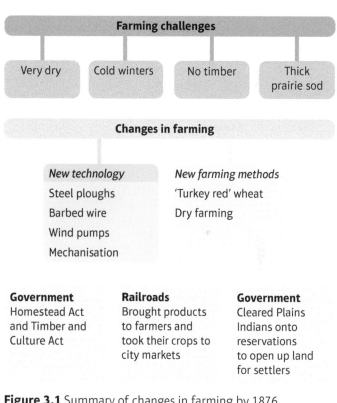

Farming challenges

| Very dry | Cold winters | No timber | Thick prairie sod |

Changes in farming

New technology	*New farming methods*
Steel ploughs	'Turkey red' wheat
Barbed wire	Dry farming
Wind pumps	
Mechanisation	

Government	**Railroads**	**Government**
Homestead Act and Timber and Culture Act	Brought products to farmers and took their crops to city markets	Cleared Plains Indians onto reservations to open up land for settlers

Figure 3.1 Summary of changes in farming by 1876.

In the period 1876–1895, the new technologies and methods shown in Figure 3.1 really began to have an impact. This impact was often enhanced by government policies and happened within the context of the industrialisation of the USA. As a result, by the 1890s, the problems facing homesteaders in the West had become manageable. Rather than being forced to adapt their lives to the challenges of the Plains environment, homestead farming was beginning to transform the Plains into rich and fertile farmland.

The impact of new farming methods

The government sponsored scientific experimentation to develop new methods to help farming in the West.

Dry farming

Dry farming was an experimental technique that aimed to conserve water in the soil. An influential method was developed by Hardy Webster Campbell, who started homesteading in Dakota Territory in 1879. Dry farming prepared the soil so that it trapped rainwater under the surface. Campbell's techniques also promoted strong root growth by crops, which meant they could access more of the water in the soil. Farmers found that dry farming worked well with wheat. Agricultural experts also promoted dry farming methods as the best way for homesteaders to farm the Plains.

Dry farming grew in popularity, but a series of severe droughts in the 1890s stopped it becoming really widespread until the start of the 20th century.

The impact of new technology

Wind pumps

The development of wind pump technology was highly significant for farming in the West. Many farmers gave up on their claims because they could not access enough water for their crops. There was plenty of water underground but, in many places, it was very deep down. There was technology to reach it, but no way to haul up enough to meet farmers' daily needs.

Wind pumps were a good solution in theory – they had been used to pump water from underground for many centuries in other parts of the world. In 1854, an engineer called **Daniel Halladay** developed a wind pump with a windmill that would swing round automatically as the wind changed direction. This was important for the Plains, which had very strong winds that frequently changed direction.

Where water was tens of metres underground, wooden windmills were strong enough to pump up the water. But, in many parts of the West, groundwater was over 100 metres down (in some places it could be 400 metres down). Also, farmers found wooden windmills often failed to stand up to winter storms. Maintaining them was expensive and time-consuming, too. Farmers had to climb up the towers every few days to oil the mechanism.

By the 1880s, efficient, all-metal windpumps that needed oiling just once a year (at ground level) had been developed. Pumping power was increased by making the windmill blades larger, setting windmills on high towers and using sophisticated geared mechanisms to convert maximum energy from the rotating blades to the water pump. Strength was added by using steel instead of wood for blades and towers. As a result, windpumps were used all over the West by both cattle ranchers and farmers. The biggest problem of farming in the West had been made manageable.

Barbed wire

First introduced in 1874, barbed wire had a huge impact on farming in the West. With timber being so scarce, barbed wire was a cheap and effective way for farmers to fence off their claims, and protect their crops and property from roaming livestock. Through the 1880s, too, cattle ranchers began to use barbed wire to keep their livestock in particular areas and to stop other people's animals from straying onto their pasture. By then, the problems of barbed wire rusting quickly and breaking had been fixed through applying a coating to the wire. New production methods also reduced its cost.

Mechanisation

Inventors and manufacturers made good money from solving farmers' problems. Many agricultural machines were developed that made farming easier and more productive. Some were specially developed to improve dry farming techniques. Dry farming required the soil to be ploughed very deeply, so what rainfall there was went deep into the soil. Improved steel ploughs were developed that could be set at the right depth for this. Then seeds needed to be planted deeply. Seed drills were developed to do this: they were drawn behind a horse, like a plough. These automatically planted seeds at the correct depth for successful dry farming.

- Mechanisation made farming faster, more efficient and more productive. It enabled farmers to farm larger areas, so successful homesteads expanded.
- Mechanisation strengthened the connection between industry and farming. Manufacturers helped farmers become more successful and, as farmers became more successful, they bought more industrial products. This boosted the US economy.

Source A

This poster from 1876 was part of a promotional campaign to publicise the benefits of barbed wire to farmers and railroad companies

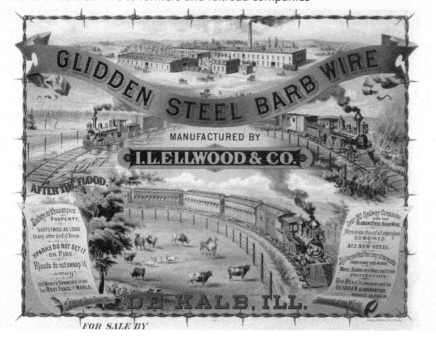

Activities

1 Select one new technology and one new farming method from Figure 3.1 (page 71). For each, explain why it was important in the development of farming in the West. Use information from previous chapters to give a full answer.

2 Make a connection between the development of farming in the West and each of the following: the railroads, government policy towards the Plains Indians, the cattle industry. For example: 'The impact of the railroads on the development of farming in the West was….'

Changes in the cattle industry

Through the 1870s, so much money went into cattle ranching that the open range became overstocked*. This situation had several serious consequences for the cattle industry in the 1880s.

- **A fall in demand:** in the eastern states, beef was so plentiful that shops had to lower their prices in order to sell the meat they had bought. This meant that the prices paid for cattle fell. By 1882, profits from cattle ranching were beginning to decrease. Ranchers kept hold of their cattle, waiting for prices to rise again.

- **Soil erosion and loss of pasture:** overstocking put a lot of pressure on the soil, damaging it. When drought hit in 1883, the grass withered, making the overstocking problem worse. Prairie fires reduced the grass cover still further.

- **The 'Great Die Up':** the winter of 1886–87 was very harsh with temperatures falling as low as –55°C. The cattle were already weakened by the consequences of overstocking; now they could not reach the grass through the deep snow and thousands died. At least 15% of open range herds perished. Many cattlemen went bankrupt.

The stock that did survive into spring 1887 was often in very poor condition, but everyone tried to sell what they had, making beef prices fall even lower. The combination of these factors put an end to ranching on the open range. The huge ranches had the most problems trying to save their cattle during the winter: the area to cover was far too large. Smaller ranches coped better, though many had to take out large bank loans to survive. Smaller ranches became the model for the cattle industry after 1887.

Key term

Overstocked*

The situation when too many livestock animals are relying on the same area of pasture: the grass gets eaten up, the soil may start to erode and animals can weaken as a result of hunger.

- Smaller herds could **easily be found** when the snows closed in and brought closer to the ranch buildings, where there was shelter and food.
- In times of drought, it was **easier to provide water** to the herd, using wind pumps to draw up water in areas without reliable surface water.
- Smaller herds were **easier to guard**, so cattlemen could start to get more control over rustling.
- Smaller herds **reduced the supply** of beef, and higher quality meat could be sold for higher prices. This enabled the cattlemen to be profitable again.
- After 1887, ranchers moved to producing **high-quality meat**. They did this by buying pure-blooded breeds of cow, like Herefords and Holsteins. These animals could not be allowed to wander freely

because breeding had to be carefully managed. Ranchers began fencing in their land with barbed wire to keep their cattle separate.

Activities ?

1. Using Figure 3.2 to help you, write a narrative account of the rise and fall of the cattle industry from the end of the Civil War to the winter of 1886–87. Use the phrases 'This was because…' or 'As a result of this…' five or more times in total (any combination is fine).

2. Did the winter of 1886–87 cause the end of the open range, or was it about to end anyway? Explain what you think and use evidence to support your answer.

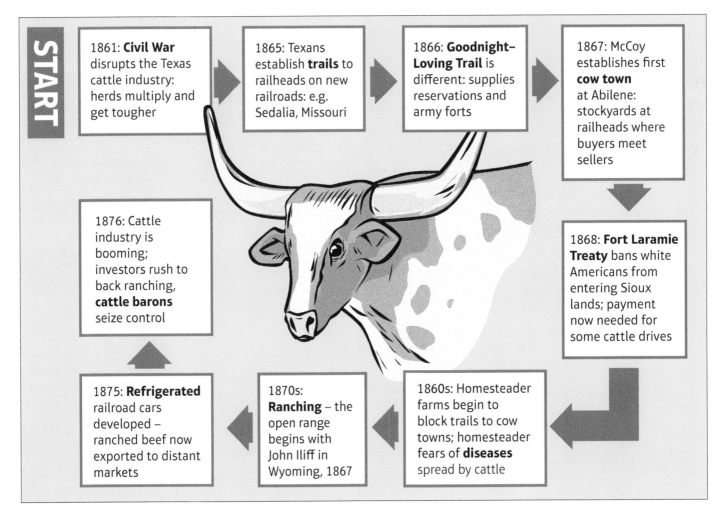

START

1861: Civil War disrupts the Texas cattle industry: herds multiply and get tougher

1865: Texans establish **trails** to railheads on new railroads: e.g. Sedalia, Missouri

1866: Goodnight–Loving Trail is different: supplies reservations and army forts

1867: McCoy establishes first **cow town** at Abilene: stockyards at railheads where buyers meet sellers

1868: Fort Laramie Treaty bans white Americans from entering Sioux lands; payment now needed for some cattle drives

1860s: Homesteader farms begin to block trails to cow towns; homesteader fears of **diseases** spread by cattle

1870s: Ranching – the open range begins with John Iliff in Wyoming, 1867

1875: Refrigerated railroad cars developed – ranched beef now exported to distant markets

1876: Cattle industry is booming; investors rush to back ranching, **cattle barons** seize control

Figure 3.2 Summary of changes in the cattle industry by 1876.

As ranchers went bankrupt, and others quit to move back east, the homesteaders moved in. This had consequences for the relationship between the remaining ranchers and farmers. There often was no pasture for livestock outside the ranch's own property – it was all fenced in by homesteaders.

Extend your knowledge

The cattle industry and the buffalo

Buffalo were able to survive the harsh winters as they were adapted to the climate but, by 1883, the buffalo had been almost completely exterminated by white hunters (see page 90). In the 1880s, some cattlemen tried breeding cows and buffalos to create an animal that could tolerate the climate extremes of the Great Plains. A more successful cross was between a Texas Longhorn and a drought-resistant Brahmin cow from India.

The impact of the end of the open range

The disastrous winter of 1886–87 was called the 'Great Die Up' because of the huge losses in the herds of the open range. It had consequences for cowboys as well as for their employers. The end of the open range meant that there was much less demand for cowboys, and those that remained in the cattle industry were employed as ranch hands.

- They now had much less adventurous lives: branding and de-horning cattle, looking after horses and calves, mending barbed wire fences, inspecting the grass in the fenced-off fields and harvesting the hay used to feed the herd during winter.

- They lived in bunkhouses, which were often not very comfortable – leaking roofs, thin walls and beds full of lice. There were schedules and rules to follow.

- They were responsible for 'riding the line': patrolling the boundary between one ranch and another.

Ranches did join together for yearly round-ups, where the cowboys rode out on the range searching for any stray cattle to be brought back for each ranch to pick out their strays and brand any calves they had found.

Activity

Draw a graph to show how the life of Texas cowboys changed between 1860 and 1890. On the *y*-axis you could plot the level of freedom that the cowboys had from 'Not at all free' up to 'Completely independent'. On the *x*-axis you could plot how difficult and dangerous their work was from 'Easy and safe' to 'Difficult and dangerous'.

Exam-style question, Section A

Explain **two** consequences of the winter of 1886–87 for the cattle industry. **8 marks**

Exam tip

Remember that the question is not asking you to describe the events of the winter of 1886–87, or the causes of the 'Great Die-Up', but instead wants an explanation of two developments that happened to the cattle industry as a result of the winter. Once you have identified each consequence, then use evidence to back up the explanation you give for each.

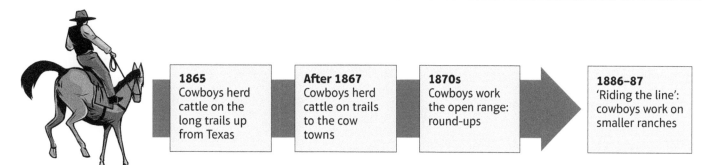

1865
Cowboys herd cattle on the long trails up from Texas

After 1867
Cowboys herd cattle on trails to the cow towns

1870s
Cowboys work the open range: round-ups

1886–87
'Riding the line': cowboys work on smaller ranches

Figure 3.3 Changes in cowboy work from the Civil War to after the winter of 1886–87.

The continued growth of settlement

For most white Americans, the settlement of the West was a natural process in which a superior race took over the land from primitive peoples as a result of **Manifest Destiny** (see page 20 for more on 'Manifest Destiny'). This vision is represented in a picture called 'American Progress', painted in 1872 and shown in Figure 3.4.

Extend your knowledge

Manifest Racism?

The ideas behind 'Manifest Destiny', were deeply racist. Treating American Indians as an inferior race allowed white Americans to tolerate inhuman treatment of American Indian peoples: a deliberate process of cheating American Indians out of their land, starving them on inadequate reservations, forcing them into conflict and murdering men, women and children.

The Exoduster movement (1879)

The Civil War between the northern anti-slavery states and the southern slave states was won by the North in 1865. When the war was won, four million slaves were freed across the USA.

However, many white people in the southern states could not accept that black Americans should be free or were capable of being free. Southern whites did everything they could to keep black Americans from becoming independent. They used violence and intimidation to stop black Americans voting. They also refused to sell land to black Americans and forced them into sharecropping*, which kept black farmers working for free on white plantation farms.

Key term

Sharecropping*

When a landowner allows a tenant to use some of their land in return for a share of the crops they grow.

The picture represents **Manifest Destiny**: white Americans' mission from God to bring light to America.

American Indians are shown running away from Progress: they are too primitive to be part of the new America. Buffalo and other wild animals are fleeing, too.

White **hunters, explorers** and **mining prospectors** lead the way West.

'Progress' is carrying a school textbook, representing education, and is unspooling **telegraph wires**. The star in her hair is called the 'Star of Empire'.

Transport progress: the American Indians have only unsaddled horses and a travois, the settlers have wagons pulled by oxen, there is a stage coach and then three lines of **railroads.**

The East is the centre of civilisation from which progress is spreading out to the West.

White **settlers** are shown making the land useful and productive: ploughing it for crops, fencing it in and building houses.

Development of white settlement

Figure 3.4 'American Progress', painted by John Gast in 1872. Other titles for the painting are 'Westward the course of destiny' and 'Manifest destiny'. The giant floating woman represents 'Progress'.

The 'Exodus'

Because the oppression of black Americans continued in the South after the Civil War, some black Americans decided to move to the West and take up Homestead Act claims to their own land. A former slave called **Benjamin Singleton** pioneered the move to Kansas. Having set up a settlement there in 1873, he promoted Kansas at meetings and in newspaper adverts in the southern states, and helped many hundreds of black Americans to move there. He helped create the foundations for an extraordinary, large-scale migration of black Americans to Kansas in 1879.

In 1879, a rumour spread that the federal government had given the whole state of Kansas to ex-slaves for them to settle. This was not true, but the rumour was significant in giving thousands of black Americans the incentive to start new lives in Kansas, causing a massive migration. By the end of 1879, 40,000 had set off west, heading for Kansas and also Missouri, Indiana and Illinois. The black settlers were called the **Exodusters**: an Exodus to the dry, dusty West.

While Singleton declared 'I am the whole cause of the Kansas immigration', his important work was in fact not the only reason for the huge scale of the migration.

- Other individuals were important too, including **Henry Adams**, who also promoted the idea of black emigration. There was widespread interest within black communities in the idea of migration generally, including migration to Liberia, a new state in Africa.

- Many black Americans had also started moving within the southern states since the Civil War, looking for better jobs and the opportunity of building new lives.

- Kansas had a historic reputation as an anti-slavery state and it became a 'free state' in 1861 – free of slavery. As a result, black Americans had reasons to believe that Kansas would welcome black people and to view the state in a positive way.

- The Homestead Act offered the promise of free land: a significant 'pull' factor for the migrants.

- The Biblical story of the Exodus also provided a religious 'push' factor: some migrants felt able to trust that God would provide for them and help them escape oppression.

Source B

'En route to Kansas': a picture from 1879, based on a sketch by H. J. Lewis that was published in *Harper's Weekly* magazine. It shows a family of Exodusters on their way to Kansas.

Impacts of the Exoduster movement

- **Impacts for settlement of the West:** by 1880, there were 43,107 black Americans in Kansas, settling 81 km² of land. Settlements, like Nicodemus in Kansas, were founded by black Americans.

- **Impacts for the black American settlers:** other settlers and ranchers had already taken all the best land in Kansas. The Exodusters were left with land in the Kansas uplands, which was very difficult to farm. Often, these settlers soon desperately needed help to survive. Also, many had come to Kansas believing that the land would be free and were not able to afford the administration fee to take up their claims. The migration had also been unplanned and charities struggled to organise help for migrants in trouble.

- **Response from Kansas government:** many Exodusters had travelled through areas affected by yellow fever and so many were dangerously ill. The Kansas governor set up an association to help the migrants, which organised colonies for them to live in and a small amount of temporary state funding to help them get started.

- **Responses from white Americans:** there was huge opposition to the Exodusters in the southern states, but most white Americans in Kansas also thought the Exodusters should not be helped and should be returned to the South. White settlers in Kansas thought it was wrong that the state government should help the Exodusters and not them.

- **End of the movement:** the reality of the situation in Kansas filtered back to the southern states and, by the 1880s, the exodus turned into a much smaller stream of migrants. These tended to have saved money and put together the resources necessary for settling in the West. Even so, Exoduster migrants typically remained poorer than the white migrants to Kansas through the 1880s and 1890s, though they were better off than they had been in the South. However, the difficulties faced by some black settlers in Kansas meant that there was a second (smaller) wave of migration out of Kansas as former Exodusters went elsewhere in the USA, especially to Nebraska and, after 1889, to Oklahoma.

Activities ?

1. How different was the Exoduster movement from other settler migrations you have studied? Identify similarities (e.g. lack of understanding of how to farm on the Plains) and differences.

2. How different was the Exoduster movement from the Mormon migration and settlement of the Great Salt Lake region (see page 22)? Identify similarities and differences.

The Oklahoma Land Rush (1893)

Indian Territory was the land that the US government had set aside for settlement by the American Indians who lived to the east of the Mississippi River and had been forcibly relocated there by the Indian Removal Act of 1830 (page 16).

Indian Territory was divided up into different sections for different tribes and, in the middle of the Territory, there was a section that was not officially allocated to a particular tribe. White settlers had been trying to move into this middle section since the start of the 1880s, but the US Army moved them off again as Indian Territory was not open to white settlement.

In 1887, the Dawes Act (see page 95) meant that, instead of the tribe owning all its land, individual Plains Indian families each received 160 acres. All the land that was left over after this was put up for general sale. Many Plains Indians then sold their family lands too, because they did not want to become farmers. Often, the Plains Indians were cheated into selling their land at a very cheap price by white land speculators.

Then, in 1889, the US government decided to open up the middle section of Indian Territory for white settlement. The land was divided up by government surveyors into 160-acre sections, and it was announced that at 12 noon on 22 April 1889, the area would be opened for claims. Thousands of hopeful settlers waited on the boundary of the unopened territory and then, once a signal was given, everyone rushed over the boundary to reach a section and claim it as theirs. This process was called a land rush.

Source C

Oklahoma Run **painted by Robert Lindneux in 1889.**

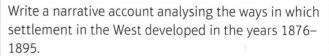

Activity ?

Study Source C. Explain what made these people so hungry for land.

There were seven land rushes in Oklahoma, starting with the land rush of 1889 (two million acres of former Indian Territory), with the last happening in 1895 (88,000 acres). The largest land rush was in 1893, when eight million acres were opened up for settlement.

Although the US government had always claimed to be protecting Plains Indian land from white Americans, this protection never lasted long. The pressure from white Americans for land to settle on was always enough for the government to give in and find ways to move the Plains Indians somewhere else, until there was nowhere left for them to live as free Plains Indians at all.

Exam-style question, Section A

Write a narrative account analysing the ways in which settlement in the West developed in the years 1876–1895.

You may use the following in your answer:

- The Exoduster movement (1879)
- The Oklahoma Land Rush (1893)

You **must** also use information of your own.   **8 marks**

Exam tip

Make sure you link the events to settlement – what difference did they make?

Summary

- Changes in farming solved most of the early problems the homesteaders had faced.
- The end of the 'open range' meant new, smaller ranches, fenced with barbed wire.
- The Exoduster movement brought black American settlers to the Plains, while the Oklahoma Land Rush opened up land to settlers from previously protected Indian Territory.

Checkpoint

Strengthen

S1 Explain which farming problem of the West was solved by wind pumps.

S2 Explain the consequences of the winter of 1886–87 for the cattle industry.

Challenge

C1 How successful were white settlers and ranchers at living on the Plains? Were they more or less successful than the Plains Indians? What factors helped or hindered them? Explain your answer.

C2 Study Figure 3.4. Put yourself in the position of Red Cloud, leader of the Oglala Sioux. What would you identify as the main consequences of 'American Progress' for your nation? Explain your answer.

How confident do you feel about your answers? Try linking up developments across all three chapters of this book – e.g. farming problems (1), tackling the problems (2) and solving the problems (3).

3.2 Conflict and tension

Learning outcomes

- Understand ways in which crime, conflict and lawlessness continued to grow in the West and how government and local communities responded to this.
- Understand how the Johnson County War of 1892 came about and its consequences.
- Understand the reasons for and impacts of the Battle of the Little Big Horn, and its consequences and implications through to the Wounded Knee Massacre of 1890.

Continued problems of law and order

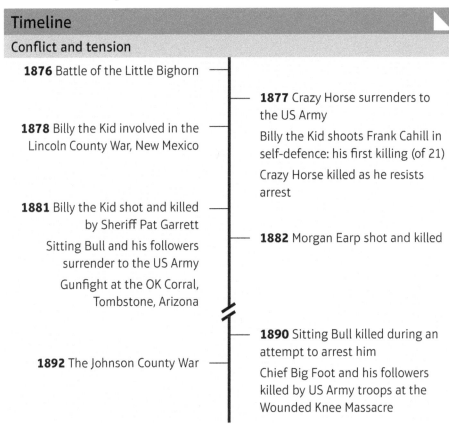

Timeline

Conflict and tension

1876 Battle of the Little Bighorn

1877 Crazy Horse surrenders to the US Army

Billy the Kid shoots Frank Cahill in self-defence: his first killing (of 21)

Crazy Horse killed as he resists arrest

1878 Billy the Kid involved in the Lincoln County War, New Mexico

1881 Billy the Kid shot and killed by Sheriff Pat Garrett

Sitting Bull and his followers surrender to the US Army

Gunfight at the OK Corral, Tombstone, Arizona

1882 Morgan Earp shot and killed

1890 Sitting Bull killed during an attempt to arrest him

Chief Big Foot and his followers killed by US Army troops at the Wounded Knee Massacre

1892 The Johnson County War

The development of the West frequently produced conflicts and tensions between people as they struggled to make a living.

- There were conflicts over the **use of resources** – between ranchers and homesteaders, for example.
- There were conflicts between **people of different races** who were now living alongside each other: between American Indians, Mexicans, Chinese, black and white Americans.

Settlements elected sheriffs and other lawmen in order to stop violence and lawlessness threatening people's livelihoods, but the justice system was influenced by these same conflicts and tensions, too. A good example is the short criminal career of Billy the Kid. Figure 3.5 shows some of the influences on his story.

Poverty
Most people struggled to make a living. Stealing was hard to resist.

Conflict over resources
There was conflict between ranchers and homesteaders, big ranchers and small ranchers, settlers and Plains Indians.

Fear and intimidation
People were afraid to act against powerful gangs: whether they were gangs of criminals or of powerful businessmen.

Independent attitudes
Men were expected to sort out their own problems, using violence if necessary. Killing in self-defence was accepted by law.

Geography
Territories were large areas with lots of places for gangs to hide from justice.

Weak justice system
Governors and law officers were often in the pay of local gangs: they were corrupt. Juries were easily influenced by local loyalties.

Problematic lawmen
There was a shortage of reliable men to step up as sheriffs and marshals. Lawmen were often former outlaws themselves.

Vigilantes
Captured criminals were often at real risk of being taken from lawmen and lynched. This undermined the idea of justice and a fair trial.

Figure 3.5 Billy the Kid and lawlessness in the West.

Billy the Kid (1859–81)

- **Early life:** Billy the Kid grew up in mining camps in New Mexico. He never held down a steady job and, when he was 14 or 15, he got into trouble for stealing butter. More thefts followed as Billy engaged in cattle rustling and horse stealing. Billy became notorious for being able to escape from jails.

- **Lincoln County War:** in 1878, Billy became involved in a conflict over resources between cattle baron John Chisum, who had a huge ranch in New Mexico, and settlers and other ranchers desperate for land. Opposition to Chisum gathered around a rancher called Murphy. Conflict broke out between the two sides, with Billy on the side fighting against Murphy.

- **Billy's private war:** although the Lincoln County War ended after Murphy's death, Billy swore to kill everyone responsible for the death of a friend in the war. He and his gang had many hideouts around the county and a lot of support from local Mexican people.

- **Law and order:** local ranchers appealed to the president to end the violence in New Mexico. He appointed a new governor. A new sheriff was also elected, with the job of bringing Billy to justice: Pat Garrett.

- **Billy's capture, escape and death:** Garrett tracked Billy down, captured him and brought him to court. The judge sentenced him to death, but the guards at the jail were careless and Billy made a dramatic, murderous escape. Garrett tracked him again to Fort Sumner and shot him dead.

Activity	?

Study Figure 3.5. How many of the factors contributing to lawlessness shown in the diagram can you find in the bullet points (above) relating to Billy the Kid?

Although Billy the Kid was a notorious thief and a murderer, he was seen as an exciting, reckless, romantic figure by many. Newspapers and cheap novels told and retold his story. He was significant in the problems of law and order for three main reasons:

1 **Powerless people** (the poor, ethnic minorities, small homesteaders and ranchers) liked the way he stood against the big northern businessmen who were dividing up America for themselves.

2 Most of his involvement in violence was as a **hired gun** in a war between cattle barons and those who dared challenge their control of the land.

3 The **justice system** in Lincoln County was too weak and corrupt to deal with Billy and his gang. Garrett said after Billy escaped from jail: 'I knew now that I would have to kill the Kid.'

Wyatt Earp and the OK Corral* (1881)

In the cow towns, cowboys often spent their money on drinking, dancing, gambling and prostitutes. Their wild, drunken behaviour was not appreciated by the northern businessmen who had come to the cow towns to make money. It was these businessmen who wanted sheriffs and marshals in their towns to keep order. They selected men like Wyatt Earp (1848–1929), who had the tough personality needed for the job.

Key term
Corral*
An enclosure for cattle or horses.

Wyatt Earp: key events

Wyatt Earp becomes a lawman after facing down rowdy cowboys	Earp first got into law enforcement in May 1874. He was involved in a fight in the cow town of Wichita and was arrested. Just then, a rowdy group of cowboys started making trouble in the town. Earp helped the deputy marshal to restore order and the mayor of Wichita offered him the job of deputy marshal. Earp moved on to be marshal in Dodge City until 1879, at which point he moved to Tombstone, Arizona Territory.
Tombstone's conflict was between big businessmen and ranchers	Tombstone was a boom town and was controlled by rich mine owners and businessmen. Against them was a faction of ranchers and cowboys, mostly from Texas, led by two ranching families: the Clantons and the McLaurys. In 1880, the rich businessmen hired Wyatt Earp as deputy sheriff to bring order to the town.
Tombstone becomes increasingly lawless	There were clashes between the Earps (Wyatt and his two brothers), and the Clantons and McLaurys, as the lawmen tried to recover stolen horses and mules. The cowboys made more trouble through 1881, rustling cattle and robbing stagecoaches. Rumours spread that the Earps had been involved in the stagecoach robberies, too: the Earps and their supporters strongly denied this.
The Earps win the gunfight at the OK Corral	In a gunfight on 26 October 1881, near Tombstone's OK Corral, the Earps killed Tom and Frank McLaury and Billy Clanton. Virgil Earp, the city marshal, claimed that he had intended only to disarm the men, but they opened fire first. Some townspeople doubted this story.
The Earps and cowboys continue to feud	Trouble continued, with the cowboys shooting Virgil and killing Morgan Earp in 1882. Wyatt shot the two men he claimed were responsible for killing his brother. Opinion turned against the Earps: their violent approach to law-keeping had only caused more conflict and Wyatt had become a murderer with no regard for the law. Wyatt and his brothers were forced to flee Tombstone.

Although business rivalries could lead to lawlessness, as in Tombstone, in general lawlessness **decreased** as settlements developed. People needed their businesses and their families to be secure. So, residents voted in town governments who passed laws to ban guns within the town limits. As a result, most towns in the West were peaceful. Even in Tombstone and Dodge City, people felt safe if they stayed out of saloons and gambling halls.

Once-lawless frontier towns were now connected to bigger towns and cities by rail and electric telegraph. This meant law officers and judges could keep in close contact with their superiors in state government, while federal government had closer links with their marshals. Consequently, the violence of Billy the Kid and the Earps was the exception rather than the rule. Residents did not want law officers like the Earps and demanded better from their government.

The range wars, including the Johnson County War

The armed conflicts between different factions for control of land in the West are known as 'range wars' after the range, the wide open Plains land that cattle roamed across. The best-known of all the range wars was the Johnson County War.

The Johnson County War was a range war between cattle barons on one side, and homesteaders and small ranchers on the other. It is significant because it shows that the West, even by the 1890s, still had places where men took the law into their own hands.

The Johnson County War (1892)
Tensions in Wyoming

In 1870, there were only 9,000 US citizens in the whole of Wyoming Territory and almost all the land was owned by the government. The Union Pacific railroad crossed the south of Wyoming in the late 1860s. Through the 1870s, huge cattle ranches developed. Rich investors, many of them British, financed the ranchers. As the population of the territory increased, wealthy, respectable cattlemen were appointed to all the key positions in government and the judiciary (judges). But, the winter of 1886–87 caused terrible losses to their herds. The power and influence of the big ranchers was shaken.

Small ranchers did better, although the big ranchers suspected this was because they had stolen many of their cows. Rustling had been a problem for many years on the open range, but now the big ranchers were struggling to survive. They used their association, the Wyoming Stock Growers Association (WSGA), to ban small ranchers that they suspected of rustling from the spring round-up.

Although the big ranchers were rich and powerful, ordinary people – homesteaders and small ranchers – were tired of the way they always grabbed everything for themselves. As a result, juries made up of ordinary people would almost never convict someone accused of rustling by the big ranchers. Big ranchers began to discuss taking the law into their own hands.

Extend your knowledge

Homesteaders in Wyoming

Wyoming, in the northern Great Plains, was very dry. Homesteaders were able to use the Desert Land Act of 1877 to claim 670 acres, which they then irrigated from water sources. 10,000 acres had been irrigated by 1884, fenced off by barbed wire. Many of these claims blocked ranchers' access to water for their livestock.

The killing of Ella Watson and Jim Averill

Ella Watson and Jim Averill farmed a homestead of 670 acres in the middle of an open-range pasture used by cattleman Albert Bothwell. Although Ella and Jim had their legal claim to the land, Bothwell wanted them gone. Disputes flared and Jim wrote a letter to a local newspaper, denouncing ranchers as nothing but rich land-grabbers. In 1889, Ella obtained a small herd of cattle. Bothwell and his men accused her of stealing his cows, seized both Ella and Jim, and hanged them. Soon after, Bothwell took over the land and Ella's cattle, too.

Other killings and murder attempts followed, leaving three owners of small ranches dead. The homesteaders and small ranchers established their own Association in 1892, and decided they would hold their own round-up a month before the WSGA's. This way, they could claim all that spring's unbranded new calves for themselves.

The invasion of Johnson County

The WSGA had had enough. It planned a full-scale invasion of Johnson County, to kill 70 men who 'should die for the good of the country'. This plan was made with the full knowledge of Wyoming's governor. The wealthy cattlemen raised a fund of $100,000 to carry it out – most of which was intended for legal fees after the killings were done. The WSGA hired 22 Texan gunmen, and paid them $5 a day plus expenses, with a bonus of $50 for every rustler they killed. They were brought into Wyoming on a train specially supplied by the Union Pacific Railroad Company.

Despite being well armed and supplied 'the Invaders' failed in their mission. Learning that two men from their hit list, Nate Champion and his partner Nick Ray, were at the KC Ranch, they abandoned their original plan and attacked the ranch instead. Nate held them off all day from the ranch's sturdy log cabin. When the Invaders set fire to the cabin, Nate ran for it but was shot down.

Word reached Sheriff Angus of Johnson County, who quickly raised a force of 40 men and went after the Invaders. Outraged citizens of Buffalo, Johnson County's main town, also joined the resistance. When a newspaper reporter asked one of them if this was because he was a rustler, the man said: 'No, but I am fighting for my home and property'. The Invaders fortified themselves at the TA Ranch, surrounded by 300 angry Johnson County residents, until the US 6th Cavalry arrived and saved them.

Source A

This photo of 'The Invaders' was taken during their arrest, in spring 1892, when they were held (in comfortable conditions) at an army fort outside Johnson County.

Extend your knowledge

'Stuart's Stranglers'

In Montana, in 1884, a vigilante campaign called 'Stuart's Stranglers' (named after Granville Stuart, a leading cattleman) targeted suspected cattle rustlers in a string of attacks that killed 19 men. Rustling activity decreased considerably after the attacks and Stuart was elected head of the Montana Stockgrowers Association. Eight years later, the Wyoming Stock Growers Association often referred to the Montana campaign as the right way to tackle the problems of cattle rustling and based their 'Invasion' on the success of Stuart's Stranglers.

The trial

The Invaders had powerful friends: the state governor, the judge, the Wyoming US marshal and two US senators supported the WSGA and its plan to end rustling.

- The governor had requested that troops be sent to the TA Ranch to prevent further bloodshed and the troops then took the Invaders away from Johnson County, despite the protests of Sheriff Angus.

- They were then taken out of the County to Fort Fetterman, in case citizens tried to lynch them.

- The best Chicago lawyers were hired by the WSGA to defend the Invaders – backed by the $100,000 fund.

- The lawyers convinced the judge that it was impossible for their clients to have a fair trial in Johnson County. The trial was moved to Cheyenne, the state capital. Jury members here were more likely to favour rich, respectable men over a bunch of rustlers.

- Knowing that Johnson County was short of money, the lawyers extended the trial as much as they could until the prosecutors had run out of money. Once the prosecution could no longer afford the trial costs, the charges against the accused had to be dropped.

Significance of the Johnson County war

Vigilante justice had been central to Frontier solutions to problems of law and order throughout the 19th century. What is more surprising is not that rich cattlemen decided it was a good idea to kill 70 men, but that so many people thought it was wrong.

Source B

An unknown local newspaper expressed its outrage at the actions of respectable, important men and state officials.

> [They] banded together in a murderous attempt to override and trample under foot every [trace] of law and order'... 'If a man murders, punish him according to law for his crime whether he be a "rustler", a cattleman or a state official.'

Reducing tensions

There were fewer tensions when both farms and ranches fenced off their land, and when ranches were based on the same property rights that homesteads were. This could not happen under the open range system but, after the winter of 1886–87, most cattlemen moved to small ranches with fenced in winter pastures.

Activities

1. The residents of Johnson County believed that the big ranchers' real reason for the war was to keep homesteaders and small ranchers off the open range. What did the big ranchers claim was the reason for the conflict? Which side do you believe? Discuss with a partner.

2. Supply endings for each of these three sentences:
   a. One consequence of the Johnson County War was...
   b. The Johnson County War was important for law and order because...
   c. The Johnson County War was important for homesteaders because...

3. In 1893, the Wyoming Stock Growers Association agreed to let small ranchers join the Association. Explain why this was important.

Conflict with the Plains Indians

From the 1830s to the 1870s, different Plains Indians tribes had agreed treaties to protect their way of life from whites with the US government, only to see those treaties fail each time. Figure 3.6 summarises key events and consequences in this process between the Californian gold rush and the end of Red Cloud's War.

The Battle of the Little Big Horn

The Battle of the Little Big Horn, in 1876, was a turning point in the history of the American West. In this battle, the US Army was defeated by the Sioux nation. The shock of this defeat transformed the US policy towards the Plains Indians. From then on, the policy was that Plains Indians had to assimilate* or die.

Key term
Assimilate*
To become like something else: for the Plains Indians, it meant becoming US citizens and rejecting all their old culture, beliefs and ways of life.

Conflict over the Black Hills

In 1874, the Northern Pacific Railroad was approaching Sioux hunting grounds in Dakota. US Army commander George Custer led an expedition of the 7th Cavalry protecting the railroad builders from Plains Indian attacks. However, Custer also used his mission to prospect for gold in the Black Hills. Within six months, thousands of prospectors followed, staking claims to land in a clear breach of the 1868 Fort Laramie Treaty.

- The US government offered to buy the Black Hills from the Sioux for $6 million, or to pay $400,000 a year for the right to mine minerals there. When this was rejected, continued Sioux raids against prospectors were used as an excuse to say that they had broken the Fort Laramie Treaty.

- Believing that the US government had betrayed them, thousands of Sioux and Cheyenne warriors left their reservations to join Sioux leaders: Sitting Bull and Crazy Horse.

- In December 1875, the government ordered the Sioux to return to their reservations. They were given 60 days to obey. After this, President Grant stated, any Sioux outside the reservations could be attacked.

- Deep snows made it impossible for all the Sioux to obey President Grant's order, even if they had wanted to. By the spring of 1876, more than 7,000 Sioux, 2,000 of whom were warriors, had erected around 1,000 lodges on lands between the Powder River and the Rosebud River. Chief Sitting Bull said: 'The whites want a war and we will give it to them.'

Events: **1848 California gold rush** means many more whites crossing Plains Indians' lands.

↓

Consequences: **1851 Fort Laramie Treaty**. Plains Indians provide safe passage across their land, and allow forts, in return for $50k a year for 50 years.

Consequences: **1851 Indian Appropriations Act**. Plains Indians to be moved onto reservations to 'protect' them from white settlers.

Events: **1859 Gold in the Rocky Mountains** means whites trespassing on Cheyenne and Arapahoe lands.

↓

Consequences: **1861 Fort Wise Treaty**. Plains Indians moved to much smaller reservations. Some Cheyenne refused to sign and refused to leave.

↓

Consequences: War with the US Army, including **1864 Sand Creek Massacre.**

Events: **1863 Gold in Montana**. Bozeman trail opened through Sioux lands in 1864, breaking Fort Laramie Treaty.

↓

Consequences: **Red Cloud's War 1866–68**.

↓

Consequences: **Fort Laramie Treaty 1868**. Great Sioux Reservation established, including the Black Hills, sacred to the Lakota Sioux.

Figure 3.6 Key events and their consequences in the conflicts over use of the Plains Indians' lands 1848–68.

Battle of the Little Bighorn (June 1876)

The US Army planned to attack the Sioux to force them back to their reservations. Custer's scouts found a camp of 2,000 warriors in the valley of the Little Bighorn. Custer only had 600 cavalrymen with him and his orders were to find the camp and then wait for reinforcements.

Custer recklessly led 200 of his men into the Little Bighorn valley. Sioux scouts reported their movements to Sitting Bull, who got the women and children of the tribes to safety while Crazy Horse led an attack. Greatly outnumbered, Custer and all his 200 men were killed.

Source C

This depiction of the Battle of the Little Bighorn is by White Bird, a Cheyenne Indian who was present at the battle. White Bird created the picture in 1894 or 1895.

Impacts of the battle

Until Little Big Horn, public opinion had been largely behind the government policy of trying to reach agreements with the Plains Indians. Little Big Horn changed public perceptions of the Plains Indians from weak savages to a real threat. If Plains Indians could beat the US Army, then what did that mean for the 'Manifest Destiny' of white America? Plains Indians would have to assimilate or die.

There was enormous pressure on the US government to crush the Plains Indian resistance. Government policy now focused on achieving this, with catastrophic impacts on Plains Indians and their way of life:

- **Plains Indians must be kept on their reservations:** army divisions pursued the Sioux and Cheyenne tribes relentlessly. Short of ammunition, food and supplies, by the end of 1876 most Sioux and Cheyenne had drifted back to their reservations. Within five years, almost all the Sioux and Cheyenne were confined to reservations, completely dependent on the US government for food and shelter.

- **Previous treaties could be ignored:** the government effectively decided that some Plains Indians had forfeited the right to have treaty deals. These Plains Indians should be moved onto smaller reservations in worse conditions than before. The Sioux were told that if they did not give up the Black Hills, the US government would stop sending them food. Faced with starvation, the Sioux gave up the Black Hills, the Powder River Country and the Big Horn mountains.

- **Military control of Plains Indians must be maintained:** the Sioux's weapons and horses were taken and they had to live under military rule. The number of soldiers and forts in the region increased.

In the spring of 1877, Crazy Horse surrendered to the US Army in Nebraska. He was killed in the autumn while under arrest at Fort Robinson. All effective resistance to the loss of their land by the Plains Indians was over.

Source D

From the *Chicago Tribune*, 7 July 1876.

```
It is time to quit this Sunday School policy,
and let Sheridan [the Commander-in-Chief
of the army in the West]... exterminate
every Indian who will not remain upon the
reservations. The best use to make of an
Indian who will not stay on a reservation
is to kill him. It is time that the dawdling
[slow and aimless], maudlin [foolishly
sentimental] peace-policy was abandoned.
```

Exam-style question, Section A

Explain **two** consequences of the Battle of the Little Bighorn (1876). **8 marks**

Exam tip

Use your knowledge of what happened to support your explanation of the effects of the battle.

Activities ?

1 Study Figure 3.6 (on page 86). Identify the key causes of conflicts with the Plains Indians.

2 Working in groups, role play the reaction to news of the Battle of the Little Bighorn amongst:

   a a family of white settlers in Nebraska

   b a warrior brotherhood of Lakota Sioux Indians

   c a company of US 7th Cavalry soldiers

   d policy makers from the US government's Bureau of Indian Affairs.

The Wounded Knee Massacre (1890)

By the end of the 1880s, the atmosphere among Plains Indians on the reservations was one of disillusionment and despair. This was heightened by a government-imposed cut in Sioux rations, coupled with a drought in the summer of 1890 that led to a failure of Sioux crops. Into this grim situation came the Ghost Dance.

The Ghost Dance

A Paiute Indian, Wovoka, claimed to have had a vision telling him that, if Plains Indians rejected white ways of life and danced a sacred dance, the Great Spirit would then bring all the dead Plains Indians back to life. A great flood would carry away the white people and the land would belong to the Plains Indians again.

The Ghost Dance spread rapidly through the reservations. President Harrison ordered the army into the reservations to take control. This was the point at which Sitting Bull was killed in an attempt to arrest him. The army wrongly believed he was planning to lead the Ghost Dancers in a rebellion.

The Wounded Knee Massacre (29 December 1890)

Sitting Bull's followers fled south and joined the band of Big Foot, another refugee from a reservation. The army caught up with them and took them to Wounded Knee Creek. A Sioux warrior resisted being disarmed and others began to dance. In the general confusion, a shot was fired. The 7th Cavalry opened fire. In ten minutes, 250 Sioux were dead. Half the dead were women and children. The Massacre was the last clash between US Army troops and the Sioux.

Source E

This photo from January 1891 shows US Army soldiers burying the dead after the Wounded Knee Massacre.

Reactions to the Wounded Knee Massacre

Public opinion of the Massacre was generally positive: soldiers who took part were praised and the public was relieved that the Ghost Dance was over.

- This reaction suggests most white Americans thought Plains Indians were naturally too wild and hostile to white settlers and that, if they could not be controlled, they should be killed.

- Public opinion and the US Army also saw Wounded Knee as revenge for the Battle of the Little Bighorn.

- Some historians argue that Wovoka's Ghost Dance movement was based on what is called **millenarian beliefs**, common amongst oppressed peoples: the dream that some supernatural event will put right all the wrongs. The fear that white Americans had of the Ghost Dance was based on the fear oppressors have: that, one day, the people they have treated so badly will rise up against them.

- In 1890, the US census office announced that the Indian Frontier had ended: nowhere within the USA's borders now belonged to any other nation or people (see page 96).

Extend your knowledge

American Indian legacy

It would be wrong to see the American Indian peoples of America as having been defeated forever. Through the 20th century, American Indians fought for their civil rights. The Massacre at Wounded Knee became a vital symbol in the American-Indian Movement.

Exam-style question, Section A

Write a narrative account analysing the conflict between the Plains Indians and the US government in the years 1876–1890.

You may use the following in your answer:

- The Battle of the Little Bighorn (1876)
- The Ghost Dance (1890)

You **must** also use information of your own. **8 marks**

Exam tip

This question is testing your knowledge and ability to write analytical narrative. Start by adding at least one more dated event to the list. You then need to describe the sequence of events in the right order (that is narrative), and you need to show how one event linked to the next and which was the most important (analysis).

Summary

- Conflicts over land continued to cause problems of law and order, especially range wars between big cattle ranchers and other land users, which also involved outlaws like Billy the Kid.
- However, in most parts of the West the government had much greater control over law and order than before, as populations increased and communications improved.
- The Johnson County War was a range war that pushed vigilante justice to an extreme that many members of the public could no longer tolerate.
- The shock caused by the 7th Cavalry's defeat to Crazy Horse at the Battle of the Little Bighorn provoked a determination to remove any threat of Plains Indian resistance to white America ever again.

Checkpoint

Strengthen

S1 Identify the key events of the Johnson County War, with the dates when they happened.

S2 Explain how the Ghost Dance was connected to the Wounded Creek Massacre.

Challenge

C1 Which of the following do you think did the most to cause conflict on the Plains: the railroads, homesteaders or gold prospecting? Back up your choice with evidence.

C2 A newspaper editorial in 1891 read: 'our only safety depends upon the total extermination of the Indians'. Do you think this is what the US government wanted to achieve? Back up your answer with evidence.

How confident do you feel about your answers? If you're not sure you answered them well, try working on them in a group. Divide up the tasks, so you can focus on investigating one aspect in depth before reporting back.

3.3 The destruction of the Plains' Indians way of life

Learning outcomes

- Understand the impact of the hunting and extermination of the buffalo on the Plains Indians' way of life.
- Understand the impact of reservations on the Plains Indians' way of life.
- Explain the significance of changing government attitudes to the Plains Indians.

The hunting and extermination of the buffalo

Timeline

The destruction of the way of life of the Plains Indians

1879 The Carlisle Indian School founded in Pennsylvania

1883 Buffalo hunters find there are no more buffalo left to kill

The Northern Pacific Railroad completed

1885 All Plains Indians are resettled onto reservations

1887 The Dawes Act divides tribal lands into family and individual plots

Source A

An old buffalo hunter, Frank Mayer, recalls a conversation with an Army officer that he had in the 1870s.

```
Mayer, there's no two ways about it, either
the buffalo or the Indian must go. Only when
the Indian becomes absolutely dependent on us
for his every need, will we be able to handle
him. He's too independent with the buffalo.
But if we kill the buffalo we conquer the
Indian. It seems a more humane thing to kill
the buffalo than the Indian, so the buffalo
must go.
```

By 1883, the once-vast herds of buffalo (25 million or more) had gone. There were opportunities for the government to stop buffalo hunting, but they chose to encourage the slaughter of buffalo instead.

Economic reasons for the extermination

- Before the 1870s, buffalo had been hunted for their warm coats, which were made into clothing. In 1871, however, a process was discovered for cheaply turning buffalo hide (skin) into just the right sort of leather for the machine belts powering US industrialisation. With prices for a buffalo hide between $1 and $3, people rushed to kill as many buffalo as they could.
- Railroads brought hunters to the Plains and transported the hides back to the cities. A very efficient process of killing was developed using powerful Sharps' rifles. Many hunters killed more buffalo than they were able to skin and some inexperienced skinners wasted a lot of hides.

Once the skin was removed, the rest of the buffalo was then just discarded to rot on the Plains. Plains Indians believed that this disrespect for the buffalo angered the spirit world and caused the buffalo to disappear.

Extermination south and north

- Hunting of the southern herd peaked in the years 1872–74, when professional buffalo hunters killed around four and a half million animals, compared to around one million killed by Plains Indians.
- The northern herd was protected by the Great Sioux reservation until 1876. As well as marking the point when the government began to break up Sioux control of the northern Plains, 1876 was also the point when the Northern Pacific Railroad reached Sioux lands and began to push west.
- In 1880, an estimated 5,000 whites (out on the Plains) were killing and skinning buffalo. By 1883, the northern herd was gone.

Extend your knowledge

Pre-existing pressures on the buffalo

The buffalo herds were already under huge pressure from repeated droughts in the 1840s and from diseases brought by cows and horses. These pre-existing factors meant that the buffalo herds in the 1870s and 1880s were weakened and vulnerable, which helps to explain why the industrialised hunting process caused such a rapid extermination.

Extermination and government policy

Exterminating the buffalo seemed to fit in well with the US government's policy of moving Plains Indians onto reservations and encouraging them to learn farming.

- Plains Indians resisted going onto reservations as long as there were buffalo to hunt. The random migrations of the buffalo herds gave Plains Indians a concept of land use that was not compatible with white settlers' ideas of a fixed, permanent property.

- Treaties gave Plains Indians the right to hunt on large areas of the Plains outside their reservations: but these had been agreed with clauses saying they would last as long as there were buffalo to hunt. Once the buffalo went, these hunting rights would end, too.

- Without their main food source, Plains Indians needed to learn to farm, and to assimilate. It also made them less independent – they had to rely on the government for food. If the government wanted to force them to do something, they could stop sending food.

- Plains Indians resisted the development of the railroads because the railroads required buffalo to be cleared from the land. Areas without buffalo made for easier railroad building.

- The extinction of the buffalo also opened up the Plains for cattle ranching. Cattle ranchers had powerful friends in the US government.

There were US citizens who were concerned about the destruction of the buffalo herds. In 1874, Congress proposed a fine of $100 for any non-American Indian to kill a female buffalo or kill more males than they needed for food, but this was blocked by President Grant.

Source B

This huge pile of buffalo skulls was photographed in the 1880s in Detroit on the way to a factory that produced fertiliser and pigment from buffalo bones.

Impact on the Plains Indians

The loss of the buffalo shattered the Plains Indians' way of life. Plains Indians had many of the skills for raising cattle and some started cattle ranching. They also began farming crops. But the cattle herds were badly affected by disease and the crops failed year after year. Reservation Indians became dependent on the government for food handouts. The government reduced the food rations to punish Plains Indians who took part in resistance resulting in starvation on the reservations. This lowered the Plains Indians' resistance to diseases like flu and measles, and many died.

Activities ?

1 Describe three differences between the way Plains Indians and whites used the buffalo.

2 Describe two consequences of the extermination of the buffalo for the Plains Indians.

3 Recreate a debate between Americans in the 1870s, who wanted to protect the buffalo, and those who thought they should not be protected. What arguments might each side have used?

The Plains Indians' life on the reservations

The US government systematically forced Plains Indians onto smaller reservations and took away their independence. Although there had been much debate about the 'Indian Problem' in the years up to 1876, by the 1880s, white American opinion was agreed that allowing Plains Indians to keep large reservations meant they tried to cling on to their old ways of life. Reservations were to be phased out and Plains Indians were to assimilate into the American way of life.

Shrinking reservations

According to the Fort Laramie Treaty of 1868, three quarters of adult male Plains Indians needed to agree to changes to the treaty terms. Although the government had forced through changes to the Sioux reservations in 1876, this had not been done with the necessary agreement. Following the Dawes Act (1887, see page 95), another round of discussions took place in 1889. The Plains Indians were again pressured into accepting further reductions in reservation size. Six small Sioux reservations were created. The surplus land from the old reservation was sold.

Taking away the power of the tribal chiefs

Signing treaties with tribal chiefs sometimes proved difficult, especially when chiefs like Sitting Bull were involved, who was determined to refuse any further loss of land. In the early 1880s, the US government set up special councils among the tribes. These councils were to take over the chiefs' powers that had enabled them to look after their people on the reservations. The US negotiators were easily able to influence council members through threats and bribes. In 1883, special courts took over the chiefs' powers to judge and punish the Plains Indians. In 1885, however, these courts were abolished in favour of the US federal law courts. This was important because it meant Plains Indians had lost all ability to govern themselves.

Government agents

Government agents used bribes of increased food rations or medical supplies in return for good behaviour amongst Plains Indian councils. A number of Plains Indians joined the Indian Agency Police, where they were fed, clothed and sheltered, and were generally able to maintain a reasonable standard of living. These Plains Indians were responsible for keeping order amongst their former tribespeople.

Education and religion

Plains Indian boys and girls were sent to schools that were off-reservation. If their parents resisted or refused, their food rations were withdrawn until they agreed. Once in school, the children lived and learned under military-style conditions. They were taught to have no respect for their traditional way of life, were brought up as Christians and were punished if they spoke their own language, or danced or kept sacred items. By 1887, 2,020 Plains Indian children were pupils at 117 boarding schools and 2,500 were in 110 day schools. One boarding school founder said that his aim was to 'kill the Indian in him and save the man'. But Plains Indians who had been educated as Americans faced prejudice from other Americans, as Source C describes.

Source C

Plenty Horses, a Brulé Sioux, was a pupil at Carlisle Indian School in Pennsylvania between 1883 and 1888, starting when he was 14. He gave the following account of his education to a reporter after he was put on trial for the murder of a US Army officer in 1891.

I found that the education I had received was of no benefit to me. There was no chance to get employment, nothing for me to do whereby I could earn my board and clothes, no opportunities to learn more and remain with the whites. It disheartened me and I went back to live as I had before going to school.

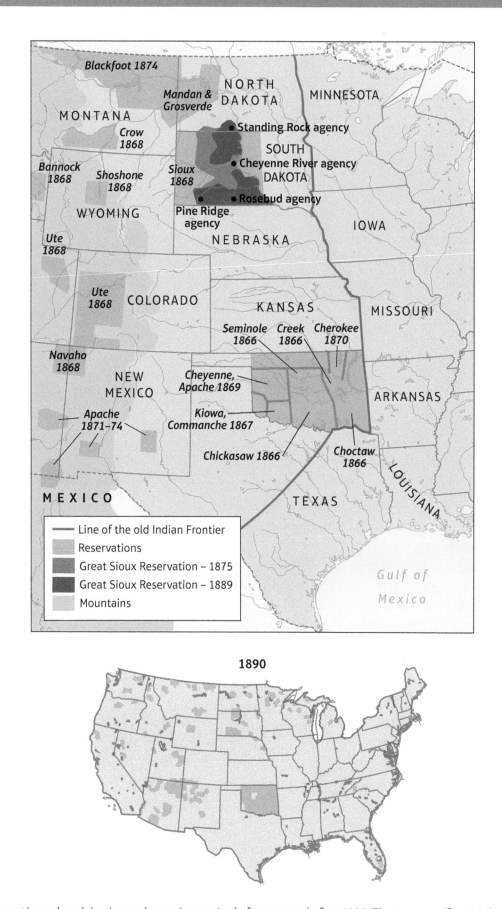

Figure 3.7 Reservations shrank in size and were increasingly fragmented after 1889. The top map (for 1889) shows the changes for the Plains Indians and the bottom map shows the situation in 1890 across the whole of the USA.

Source D

Two photographs of the same three Lakota Sioux boys. The one on the left was taken when they arrived at Carlisle Indian School in Pennsylvania in 1879. The one on the right was taken six months later.

Living conditions

Exterminating the buffalo herds and reducing the reservation size to small fragments meant the economic basis of life for Plains Indians was undermined.

- A nomadic hunting existence was no longer permitted and Plains Indians no longer had the ability to feed, clothe and shelter themselves.
- Farming was not a part of traditional American Indian life for most Plains tribes. They did not have the skills needed to farm the Plains. For some nations, such as the Pawnee, the change was not so dramatic, because they were farmers as well as hunters. Even so, the reservations were mostly on poor land. Crops failed due to droughts, pests and diseases.
- Dependence on the government for food and clothing increased. Disease, alcoholism and depression spread through the reservations.

Despite the social problems created by reservations, the government still continued to believe that breaking up Plains Indian society would eventually mean the Plains Indians stopped relying on the government.

Source E

In 1882, Chief Sitting Bull gave an interview to a journalist while he and his family were being held at Fort Randall. As part of this interview, he said the following.

The life my people want is a life of freedom. I have seen nothing that a white man has, houses or railways or clothing or food, that is as good as the right to move in the open country, and live in our fashion.

Activities ?

1 Using Source C and Source D to help you, write a diary account for one of the Lakota boys describing how different life was at the Carlisle Indian School compared to their life amongst the Lakota.

2 President Grant's Peace Policy (1868) promised peace on the reservation and war outside of them. Analyse how the US government policy towards reservations changed after 1876.

3 Explain why white Americans did not agree with Sitting Bull (Source E) about what was best for his people.

Changing government attitudes to the Plains Indians

Government attitudes towards the Plains Indians had often changed in the years since the Permanent Indian Frontier was set up c1834. Sometimes government policy was most influenced by those who wanted the Plains Indian threat to be exterminated: for example, after the Battle of the Little Bighorn in 1876. At other times, the government was influenced by those who believed Plains Indians could assimilate into American society, given time.

The government had chosen a policy of reservations for the Plains Indians in order to keep them away from white settlers. The reservations had been set up and were protected by US law through treaties. The treaties were signed by chiefs, as representatives of the Plains Indian tribes.

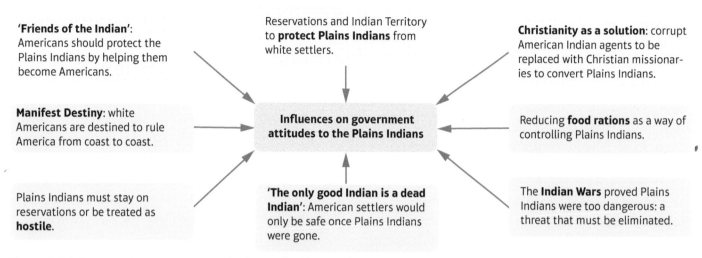

'Friends of the Indian': Americans should protect the Plains Indians by helping them become Americans.

Reservations and Indian Territory to **protect Plains Indians** from white settlers.

Christianity as a solution: corrupt American Indian agents to be replaced with Christian missionaries to convert Plains Indians.

Manifest Destiny: white Americans are destined to rule America from coast to coast.

Influences on government attitudes to the Plains Indians

Reducing **food rations** as a way of controlling Plains Indians.

Plains Indians must stay on reservations or be treated as **hostile.**

'The only good Indian is a dead Indian': American settlers would only be safe once Plains Indians were gone.

The **Indian Wars** proved Plains Indians were too dangerous: a threat that must be eliminated.

Figure 3.8 Influences on government attitudes to the Plains Indians.

By the late 1880s, much had changed. The Plains Indian way of life had been destroyed by unsustainably-sized reservations with few animals to hunt. The political power of the chiefs to govern their people had been removed. Plains Indians' own beliefs were suppressed in favour of instruction about Christianity and Plains Indian children were educated off-reservation in 'civilised' behaviour. But, despite providing incentives for Plains Indians to become civilised farmers, most seemed to sink into poverty and sickness, surviving on government handouts. To many would-be settlers, this seemed unfair: why did Plains Indians still have land that they were not using profitably?

The government decided that the reservation system was causing the problem. Plains Indians still lived as part of a tribe, not as individuals. Although the chiefs had no political power, their people still looked up to them. The chiefs only wanted things to go back to how they had been, which made them resist any further changes. The tribes shared work and food between them instead of competing against each other to have the most land, make the most money and own the most things, like white people did.

The Dawes Act (1887)

The Dawes Act of 1887 was like a Homestead Act for Plains Indians. Each Plains Indian family was allotted a 160-acre share of reservation land. Single Plains Indians were allotted 80 acres and orphans under 18 got 40 acres. Plains Indians who took up the offer and left the reservation, could then become American citizens. The

Act was only passed in Congress once something else was added: all the reservation land left over could be sold to whites. This land was often bought by railroad companies and land speculators.

The aims of the Dawes Act were to:

- break up the power of the tribe and tribal chiefs, and encourage individualism
- encourage individual families to farm for themselves, rather than relying on the tribe
- encourage Plains Indians to assimilate and become American citizens
- free up more land for settlers
- reduce the cost to the federal government of running the reservation system.

Significance of the Dawes Act

The policy worked in freeing up more land for settlers. The result of the Dawes Act was that, by 1890, Plains Indians had lost half of the lands they still had in 1887 to whites. Those that took up allotments often found it impossible to make a living farming on the Plains: the conditions were too tough, the soil too poor and the amount of land too little. Most gave up, sold their land to whites and ended up landless. Those who kept it then passed it on to their children, dividing the land up into smaller plots. These smaller plots made farming even harder than before. Many Plains Indians were also cheated out of their land by whites. As a result, life for Plains Indians became even harder in conditions that were even worse than before.

Closure of the Indian Frontier

In 1890, the US census office declared the Frontier was closed (in other words, it ceased to exist). Settlement of the West had been so rapid that 'there can hardly be said to be a frontier line' between white settled land and the 'wilderness'. There were enough settlers for new states to be established in the West, such as North Dakota, South Dakota, Montana, Idaho and Wyoming. Railroads criss-crossed the West and cities had grown up, including mining towns and cow towns. The USA's first national park was also established, to protect wilderness areas – Yosemite, in 1890. It was almost as though white Americans wanted to keep a little piece of the West untouched, to remind them of what they had achieved, and what had been lost.

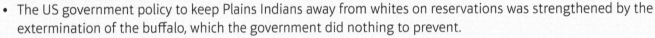

Activities   **?**

1   Explain how government attitudes to the Plains Indians changed between 1876 and 1887.

2   Removals, Treaties, Reservations and Homesteads. Use these headings in a timeline listing the different government policies towards the Plains Indians from c1834 to 1887.

3   President Cleveland, who introduced the Dawes Act, once said that the people should support the government; the government should not support the people. What were the consequences of this view for the Plains Indians?

Summary

• The US government policy to keep Plains Indians away from whites on reservations was strengthened by the extermination of the buffalo, which the government did nothing to prevent.

• Reservation life was extremely tough and, by the 1880s, people within the government had come to believe that the Plains Indians could only be 'saved' if the reservation system was ended.

• The Dawes Act of 1887 did not achieve its aims of encouraging Plains Indians to become independent homesteaders and American citizens. By the time the Frontier was closed in 1890, Plains Indians had lost half the land they had in 1887.

Checkpoint

Strengthen

S1 Explain the importance of the buffalo to the Plains Indians.

S2 Describe the ways the US government used politics, food, religion and education to control Plains Indians on reservations.

Challenge

C1 Explain three consequences of the Dawes Act for the way of life of the Plains Indians.

C2 Identify the pressures that influenced the US government policy towards the Plains Indians. Figure 3.8 on page 95 will help.

How confident do you feel about your answers? If you are not sure you answered them well, go back to the text in this section to find the details you need.

Recap: Conflicts and conquest, c1876–c1895

Recall quiz

1 In which year was the terrible winter that meant the end of the open range?

2 Who was the leader of the 7th Cavalry when they were defeated by Crazy Horse in 1876?

3 What was the name given to the religious cult of the 1890s that looked to the Great Spirit to restore the Plains Indians' way of life to them?

4 In what year did hunters realise that there were no more buffalo to hunt?

5 In 1892, a range war broke out in which county of Wyoming?

6 The Sioux called them Paha Sapa: what was the English name for the sacred hills where gold was discovered in 1874, triggering the Sioux Wars?

7 Which two ranching families were Wyatt Earp and his brothers in conflict with in Tombstone, Arizona in 1881?

8 Which state did most Exodusters migrate to?

9 Which lawman caught Billy the Kid, saw him escape and then shot him in 1881?

10 In which year did the US census office declare the Frontier was closed?

Activities ?

1 Continue a timeline of your American West studies. Use this chapter to note down key dates for your timeline. You should start from 1876 and end in 1895.

2 Create Snap cards for the American West: each one a key feature or key event from the period (1830s–1895). Each player plays a card face up at the same time. The first person to make a valid link between the two cards wins the pair. Some example cards are shown on this page.

3 Thinking about everything you have learned in this chapter, which one event would you argue was the most significant for the settlement of the American West in the period from 1876 to 1895? Explain the choice you have made.

Exam-style question, Section A

Explain **two** of the following:

• The importance of the Battle of the Little Bighorn (1876) for government attitudes towards the Plains Indians.

• The importance of the Johnson County War (1892) for law and order in the West.

• The importance of the Oklahoma Land Rush of 1893 for settlement of the West.

16 marks

Exam tip

This question is testing your ability to explain how and why an event is significant. A strong answer would explain two or three consequences of the event and contain relevant factual knowledge. The best answer will also be organised and flow smoothly, something you can achieve by using 'linking' phrases like 'It was also important because it led to…' or 'Thirdly, it meant that…'.

Writing historically: narrative analysis

When you write a narrative analysis, you need to explain a series of events: their causes and consequences. You need to think about how you express the links between **causes** and **effects**.

Learning outcomes

By the end of this lesson, you will understand how to:

- use conjunctions to link and indicate the relationship between points
- use non-finite verbs to link relevant information or indicate the relationship between points.

Definitions

Co-ordinating conjunction: a word used to link two clauses of equal importance within a sentence, e.g. 'and', 'but', 'so', 'or', etc.

Subordinate clause: a clause that adds detail to or develops the main clause, linked with a subordinating conjunction such as 'because', 'when', 'if', 'although', etc.

How can I link my points in sentences to show cause and effect?

When explaining a complex sequence of events, use **co-ordinating conjunctions** to link them in sentences.

1. Look at this exam-style narrative analysis task:

> Write a narrative account analysing the conflict between the Plains Indians and the US government in the years 1876-1890. **(8 marks)**

How could you link these three points using just co-ordinating conjunctions, e.g. 'and', 'but', 'so'?

In 1874, the Northern Pacific Railroad was approaching Sioux hunting grounds in Dakota.

Custer used his mission of protecting the rail workers to prospect for gold in the Black Hills.

Thousands of prospectors swarmed all over the Black Hills.

2. You can also use **subordinating** conjunctions to make the relationship between cause and effect clear. For example, linking:

- an explanation: (e.g. 'because', 'as', 'in order that', etc)
- a condition: (e.g. 'if', 'unless', etc)
- a comparison: (e.g. 'although', 'whereas', 'despite', etc)
- a sequence: (e.g. 'when', 'as', 'before', 'after', 'until', etc.)

Look at these simple, short questions and answers:

a. Why did the government claim the Plains Indians had broken the Fort Laramie Treaty? *Government attempts to buy the land were refused and Plains Indian raids continued.*

b. What caused thousands of Plains Indians to leave their reservations? *They believed the government had betrayed them, breaking the Fort Laramie Treaty.*

c. What was the result of the government demand that the Plains Indians return? *Winter weather largely prevented them doing so, meaning that they were declared hostile.*

d. Why did Custer lose at Little Big Horn? *He was badly outnumbered and failed to wait for reinforcements.*

Rewrite the information in each question and answer as a single sentence. Choose a different type of subordinating conjunction (explanation, condition, comparison and sequence) in each one to express the relationship between cause and effect as clearly as possible.

3. Experiment with different ways of using a subordinating conjunction to link two or more of your sentences into a single sentence.

How can I link my points in other ways?

You can add relevant information and further explanation of cause and effect using **non-finite verbs**. These include present participles and past participles: facing / faced, determining / determined, cutting / cut.

Compare these two extracts, written in response to the exam-style question on the previous page:

> The US government had to change its approach because it was faced with great public pressure after Little Big Horn.

Two points are linked using a subordinating conjunction.

> Faced with great public pressure after Little Big Horn, the US government had to change its approach.

Two points are linked using a non-finite verb.

Look at the two sentences below. How could you link the two points in each one, using a non-finite verb instead of a conjunction? **Hint:** think about how you could use a non-finite form of the highlighted verb.

> Wovoka was determined to encourage Plains Indians to resist reservation life, so he began the Ghost Dance.
>
> Sitting Bull was killed in a clumsy attempt to arrest him when US troops were ordered into the reservations to restore control.

Did you notice?

There are lots of different ways to link points in sentences. Some of them make the relationship between points more clearly than others. Choose **one** of the sentences above. Experiment with rewriting it in two or three different ways, using different methods to link points. Which version expresses the relationship most clearly and fluently?

Improving an answer

Now look at this paragraph from the beginning of one student's response to the exam-style narrative analysis task on the previous page:

> Sitting Bull's followers fled south to escape the army and joined Big Foot. The army caught up with them and took them to Wounded Knee Creek. A Sioux warrior resisted being disarmed and others began to dance. A shot was fired. The 7th Cavalry opened fire with repeating rifles and machine guns. 250 Sioux and 25 soldiers died.

4. Try rewriting this paragraph, using conjunctions and non-finite verbs to make the sequence of events, and the relationship between cause and effect, clear.

5. Continue the response above with a second paragraph explaining how the situation developed. Use conjunctions and non-finite verbs to make clear connections between causes and effects.

Writing analytical narrative

The difference between a story and a narrative account that analyses

Paper 2, Question 2 will ask you to 'Write a narrative account analysing…' (see page 102 in *Preparing for your exams*). You are not being asked to tell a story in the examination; you are being asked to explain how events led to an outcome. This means showing that the events are a series of happenings that have links between them. To do this, you must show that:

- events are prompted by something
- these events react with other events (or perhaps they react with existing circumstances)
- consequences follow from them.

Showing links like these is what turns a story into 'an account that analyses'.

Narratives for young children are always stories; they deal with events and descriptions. For example, many versions of the adventures of Toad of Toad Hall have been published. These narratives show how Toad got himself into a number of scrapes. One episode describes his fixation with acquiring a fast car, his theft of one, his arrest for dangerous driving and his subsequent trial and imprisonment.

Here are some extracts from the story.

Toad steals a motor car

Toad had a passion for cars. He saw a car in the middle of the yard, quite unattended. Toad walked slowly round it. 'I wonder,' he said to himself, 'if this car starts easily.' Next moment he was turning the starting handle. Then he heard the sound of the engine and, as if in a dream, he found himself in the driver's seat. He drove the car out through the archway and the car leapt forward through the open country... .

This extract has the first important ingredient of narrative: sequence – putting events in the right order. Words and phrases like 'next moment' and 'then' show the sequence. However, it lacks the analytical links between events. In this case, key **links** could be built around phrases such as 'because', 'in order to' or 'as a result of this'.

For example:

Toad saw the car parked in the middle of the yard. Because there was no one with it, he took the opportunity to have a good look at it. He even gave the starting handle a turn in order to see how easily it started. It started easily, but the sound of the engine affected Toad so much that his old passion for cars resurfaced and his urge to drive the car increased to such an extent that it became irresistible. As a result, as if in a dream, he found himself in the driver's seat...

The analytical narrative, as well as linking events, also makes clear what followed on from them – what difference they made. It uses **process** words and phrases that show something was happening. In this example, the process words and phrases are 'affected', 'resurfaced', 'increased' and 'became'.

Activities ?

1. Choose a story that you know well – or think of a plot for a story of your own.

2. Select up to eight key events in the story and list them in a sequence. Ideally, these events should be from the beginning, middle and end of the story; (if two things happen at the same time you can list them together). Create a flow chart with arrows from one event to the next in the sequence. Label your arrows with links chosen from the chain of linkages (see Figure 1).

3. Write a narrative account analysing the key events of your story. Use the links and at least five process words. Choose them from the process word case (see Figure 2) or use others of your own. Remember that events can combine with long-standing feelings or circumstances as part of the narrative (for example, Toad's passion for motorcars).

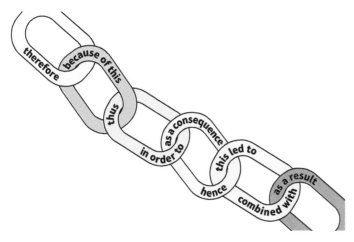

Figure 1 The chain of linkages.

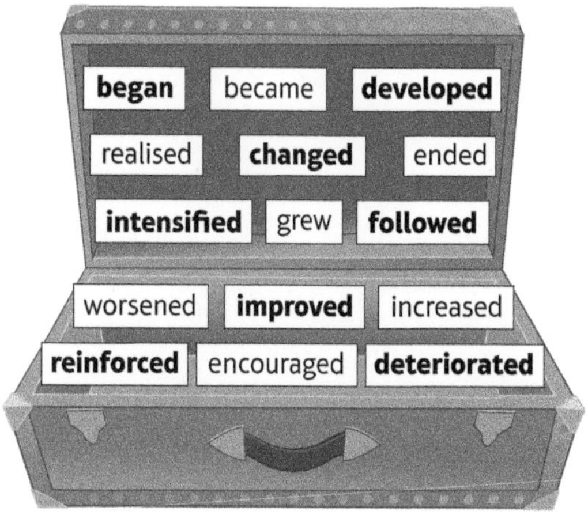

Figure 2 Process word case.

Writing historical accounts analysing…

You may be asked to write an account that analyses the key events which led to something, or the key events of a crisis, or the way in which something developed. This example has shown the skills you will need to write a good historical account. As you prepare for your examination, you should practise by:

- selecting key events
- sequencing them
- linking them into a process that explains an outcome.

As you study the events of the American West, c1835–c1895, note the linking phrases and process words the author has used in this book. You should add them to your own lists. When you create your own analytical historical narratives, try to make use of both linking phrases and process vocabulary.

Activities ?

Study the timeline on page 49. You can use the events from it to help you to answer the following question:

Write a narrative account analysing the key events of the growth of the cattle industry, 1861–70.

1 With a partner, write the events on pieces of card, without their dates, and then:

   a practise sequencing them correctly

   b agree on another one or two events you could choose to include in your account and any events you could remove

   c identify an instance where long-standing circumstances (or attitudes) were involved as events unfolded.

2 Working individually, write your own narrative account, with linkages and showing a process. Focus on what it is you are explaining and choose process words which relate to the growth of the cattle industry, e.g. extended, expanded and created.

3 Either swap accounts with a partner or check your own account. Highlight linkages in yellow and process words in green. You can use the same words more than once, but aim to have at least five green and five yellow highlights. See if using more 'process words' improves your account even more.

You are now ready to complete your exam question. Remember to use **SSLaP**.

- **S**elect key events and developments.
- **S**equence them in the right order.
- **L**ink them, **a**nd
- Show the **P**rocess that led to the outcome of your analytical narrative.

Preparing for your GCSE Paper 2 exam

Paper 2 overview

Your Paper 2 is in two sections that examine the Period Study and British Depth Study. They each count for 20% of your History assessment. The questions on The American West, c1835–c1895 are in the Period Study and are in Section A of the exam paper. You should use just under half the time allowed for Paper 2 to write your answers to Section A. This will give you a few moments for checking your answers at the end of Section B.

History Paper 2	Period Study and British Depth Study			Time 1 hour 45 mins
Section A	Period Study	Answer 3 questions	32 marks	50 minutes
Section B	Depth Options B1 or B2	Answer 3 questions	32 marks	55 minutes

Period Study Option 24/25: The American West, c1835–c1895

You will answer Questions 1, 2 and 3.

1 Explain two consequences of... (2 x 4 marks)

Allow ten minutes to write your answer. Write about each consequence. You are given just over half a page for each. Use this as a guide for answer length. You should keep the answer brief and not try to add more information on extra lines. This will make sure you allow enough time for later questions worth more marks. Make sure you focus on consequence: *as a result; as a consequence; the effect was* are useful phrases to use.

2 Write a narrative account analysing... (8 marks)

This question asks you to write a narrative explaining how events led to an outcome. Allow 15 minutes to write your answer. You are given two information points as prompts to help you. You do not have to use the prompts and you will not lose marks by leaving them out. Always remember to add in a new point of your own as well. Higher marks are gained by adding in a point extra to the prompts. You will be given at least two pages of lines in the answer booklet for your answer. This does not mean you should try to fill all the space. The front page of the exam paper tells you 'there may be more space than you need'. Aim to write an organised answer, putting events in the right order and showing how one connects to the next. Your narrative should have a clear beginning, middle and end.

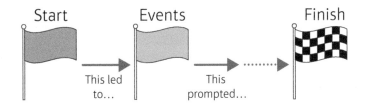

3 Explain the importance of two... (2 x 8 marks)

This question is worth half your marks for the whole Period Study. Make sure you have kept 25 minutes of the exam time to answer. It asks you to explain the importance of events and developments. You have a choice of two out of three. Take time to make the choice. Before you decide, be clear what you have to explain: the question is always worded as 'Explain the importance of... for... .' It is a good idea during revision to practise identifying the importance of key events **for** something: what did they affect or lead to? Ask yourself: 'What difference did they make to it?' or 'Why did they matter?' Be clear about your reasons for saying something is important.

Paper 2, Question 1

Explain **two** consequences of the introduction of barbed wire in the West (1874). (**8 marks**)

Exam tip

The question wants you to explain the results of something. What difference did it make? Use phrases such as 'as a result' or 'the effect of this was'.

Average answer

Consequence 1:
Barbed wire was invented in 1874 by Joseph F. Glidden, who improved on an earlier idea for using wire instead of wood for fences. Because barbed wire has spikes on it cattle stay away from it, but there was conflict between homesteaders and cattlemen as a result of using barbed wire.

This general information about barbed wire is correct but it is not being used to explain consequences. Saying that barbed wire led to the conflict is too vague.

Consequence 2:
Barbed wire was also used by homesteaders to fence in their plots. They needed fences to keep their own livestock off their crops and also to keep other people's livestock off their crops. The consequence was that it made farming easier.

This is correct but, again, too general and vague. We need to know why homesteaders struggled to fence crops before 1874 and what the consequences therefore were of its introduction.

Verdict

This is an average answer because it identifies two consequences with some support, but it needs more explanation of consequence with specific information.
Use the feedback to rewrite this answer, making as many improvements as you can.

Paper 2, Question 1

Explain **two** consequences of the introduction of barbed wire in the West (1874). (**8 marks**)

Exam tip

The question wants you to explain the results of something. What difference did it make? Use phrases such as 'as a result' or 'the effect of this was'.

Strong answer

Consequence 1:
A consequence of homesteaders' use of barbed wire was that it caused problems for the cattle industry. Because homesteaders' claims usually included a water source, fences often prevented cattlemen's open-range cows from reaching water. So a consequence of barbed wire was conflict between homesteaders and cattle ranchers. This became worse when ranchers moved to smaller, enclosed ranches: now ranchers used it to fence off their winter pastures, often preventing new homesteaders' gaining access to water sources for their livestock.

This is a better consequence to use than making a general claim that barbed wire led to conflict. The answer could have included information on wire cutting to give further evidence of conflict.

Consequence 2:
Importing timber to use for fencing was very expensive, but homesteaders needed to fence off their crops to protect them from animals. They also needed to fence their own livestock to keep it away from other animals that might be carrying disease. The consequence of barbed wire was that it solved this problem of a lack of timber on the Plains. Large areas of land could be fenced effectively and cheaply.

Good use of detail that is specific to the period and relevant to the question. Setting out the problem before the introduction of barbed wire has made the consequence much easier to explain.

Verdict

This is a strong answer because two clear consequences are now provided, and are backed up by relevant, specific information.

Paper 2, Question 2

Write a narrative account analysing the key events in the years 1851–66 that led to the beginning of Red Cloud's War. You may use the following in your answer:
- the Fort Laramie Treaty (1851)
- the discovery of gold in Montana

You **must** also use information of your own. **(8 marks)**

Exam tip

Remember that the key to scoring well on this type of question is to explain how one event leads to the next in a logical and structured way.

Average answer

6th

Red Cloud's War began in 1866 after the US Army began building forts in lands that had been granted to the Sioux by the Fort Laramie Treaty in 1851.

The forts were built by the US Army to protect whites travelling across Sioux hunting lands along the Bozeman Trail to newly-discovered goldfields in Montana. The government had ordered the army to protect the travellers, even though they were breaking the Fort Laramie Treaty. Again and again the discovery of gold caused these invasions of Plains Indian territory, and the US government always backed white Americans against the Plains Indians. This was the major cause of tension between the US government and the Plains Indians, leading to Red Cloud's War.

The most important cause of Red Cloud's war was therefore the discovery of gold in Montana. This led to the creation of a new trail across the Sioux's hunting grounds, which broke the Fort Laramie Treaty of 1851. Enraged by this, the Sioux attacked the whites and the US government sent in the army to protect the travellers, escalating tensions. When the army started to build forts, the war began.

This introduction to the answer uses accurate information but it could be improved with a clear starting point to the narrative: the first Fort Laramie Treaty.

Instead of writing about causes of the war, the student should have identified key events leading up to the war and analysed the ways these events linked together to produce an outcome: the war.

The student has listed some key events here and started to look at the links between them, but not in enough depth and still with the aim of identifying causes, which is not the right approach here.

Verdict

This is an average answer because:
- the student should have identified key events leading up to the war
- these events should have been set out in a logical order (the order in which they happened is usually the best approach) and the student should have considered the ways in which one event related to the next.

Use the feedback to rewrite this answer, making as many improvements as you can.

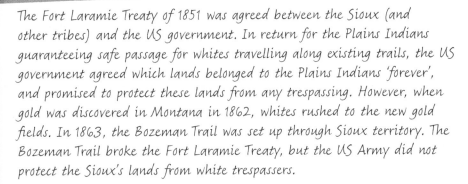

Write a narrative account analysing the key events in the years 1851–66
that led to the beginning of Red Cloud's War. **(8 marks)**

Strong answer

The Fort Laramie Treaty of 1851 was agreed between the Sioux (and
other tribes) and the US government. In return for the Plains Indians
guaranteeing safe passage for whites travelling along existing trails, the US
government agreed which lands belonged to the Plains Indians 'forever',
and promised to protect these lands from any trespassing. However, when
gold was discovered in Montana in 1862, whites rushed to the new gold
fields. In 1863, the Bozeman Trail was set up through Sioux territory. The
Bozeman Trail broke the Fort Laramie Treaty, but the US Army did not
protect the Sioux's lands from white trespassers.

> The student has identified the first events in their narrative. Giving accurate dates for events helps structure the narrative.

As a result of this betrayal of the Fort Laramie Treaty, furious Sioux
warriors demanded that whites turn back. They also attacked them. This
led to the US government saying that the Plains Indians had broken the
treaty, too. Because of this, in 1865, the US Army was ordered into the
area to protect the white travellers.

> Links are made between key events, e.g. the Bozeman Trail broke the Fort Laramie Treaty, and the consequences that followed from this.

In order to try to get what it wanted from the Sioux without a fight,
the US government organised a peace council in 1866. The government
negotiators wanted white settlers to be allowed safe passage along the
Bozeman Trail, and for new forts to be built along the trail to 'protect'
Plains Indian lands. Red Cloud was at the council, speaking as a chief of
the Oglala Sioux. He refused to allow the Bozeman Trail or the forts. His
experience of the Fort Laramie Treaty showed him that the government was
not to be trusted.

> By writing linking phrases like 'in order to', 'despite' and 'as a consequence', the student has signposted their analysis.

Despite his refusing to allow the forts, Red Cloud learned that soldiers
had started building them anyway. As a consequence, Red Cloud left the
council, certain that the Sioux must defend their lands by force. Red
Cloud's first attack was at a newly-built fort, leading to Fetterman's Trap:
the US Army's worst defeat against the Plains Indians to that point. Red
Cloud's War had begun.

Verdict

This is a strong answer because:
- key events are identified
- these events are structured in a logical order
- the student has analysed how the consequences of the events linked together to produce the outcome – Red Cloud's War.

Paper 2, Question 3

Explain **two** of the following:
- The importance of cattle trails for the development of the cattle industry in the 1860s.
- The importance of the railroads for changes in the way of life of the Plains Indians.
- The importance of the wagon trails for the early settlement of the West. **(16 marks)**

Exam tip

In the exam, you will have two separate answer sheets in the booklet for this question, one for each of the two answers you give in Question 3. Make sure you indicate at the start of each answer which point you are addressing: you are prompted to do this.

Average answer

6th

In the Civil War, in the years 1861-65, the longhorn herds of cattle increased in Texas and they were not worth much money. After the Civil War, there was high demand for beef in the northern cities. Goodnight and Loving made the first Long Drive after the Civil War to Fort Sumner. They sold the cattle to feed the reservations.

Cattle trails were very important to the cattle industry because cowboys herded large herds of cattle up the trails from Texas to the railheads in Kansas and Missouri. Animals worth $5 in Texas could be sold for $40 in Chicago. The Chisholm Trail was also important because there was grassland along most of it so the cattle did not lose so much weight on the trail.

The completion of the First Transcontinental Railroad in 1869 was important because now the USA was connected from east to west. The cattle industry also developed because of railroads, with cow towns like Abilene growing up at railheads. All this meant more whites travelling across the Plains and that was not good for the Plains Indians.

The railroad also brought industrial products from big cities to settlers on the Plains, such as farm machinery and barbed wire. The railroads also took the farmers' crops back to the cities so they could be sold, so more farmers moved onto land the Plains Indians used for hunting.

The railroad was very bad for the Plains Indians because it meant that all the buffalo were killed. The trains brought hunters to the Plains, like Wild Bill Cody (Buffalo Bill).

The student uses relevant points to describe the use of cattle trails and the long drives. The student frequently says that cattle could be sold for profit, but does not explain the importance of the trails to the development of the cattle industry.

The point is correct, but needs more explanation of the impact on the way of life of the Plains Indians.

These two paragraphs include good details about the importance of railroads, but their impact on the way of life of the Plains Indians has not been developed.

Verdict

This is an average answer because:
- more development is needed
- in the second answer, the student does not connect points to importance.

Use the feedback to rewrite this answer, making as many improvements as you can.

Paper 2, Question 3

Explain **two** of the following:

- The importance of cattle trails for the development of the cattle industry in the 1860s.
- The importance of the railroads for changes in the way of life of the Plains Indians.
- The importance of the wagon trails for the early settlement of the West.
  (16 marks)

One development is demonstrated below but a strong answer would have to explain a **second** choice as well.

Strong answer

The railroads were an important part of encouraging settlement and therefore challenged the Plains Indians' way of life in their traditional areas. The 1862 Pacific Railroad Act gave railroad companies grants of land surrounding the railroad routes. This land had previously been behind the Permanent Indian Frontier and was now sold to settlers. When finished, the railroads enabled more settlers to travel to the Plains and made the transport of machinery and raw materials possible. This further encouraged settlers to farm in the Great Plains and settlers started to demand more land.

More pressure on land in the West was created by the development of cow towns at railheads, such as Sedalia and Abilene, and ranching on the Plains. As a result, the Plains Indians' reservations were, bit by bit, made smaller. Railroads were also used by gold prospectors who trespassed on Plains Indian hunting grounds (e.g. in the Black Hills in Dakota) and were even used to transport troops who gave the prospectors protection. The Plains Indians were also forced by the US Army to stay on their reservations to avoid conflict with settlers. These restrictions were very difficult for nomadic people.

The Plains Indians' way of life depended on the buffalo. The railroads had a major impact on their way of life because they brought white hunters and skinners to the Plains who exterminated first the southern and then the northern herds. Buffalo hides were transported by train from the Plains to factories for processing. Without buffalo to hunt, Plains Indians lost their source of food, clothing and shelter. They lost the nomadic life of following the buffalo herds, and men lost their role as hunters. Their lives changed towards having to rely on government handouts of food, and to farming and ranching instead of hunting.

The railroads intensified the threats to the Plains Indians' way of life. Once the railroad was built, increasing numbers of whites followed: prospecting, hunting buffalo or settling the land. All three of these things combined to put pressure on the Plains Indians to move onto reservations where their nomadic and independent way of life was undermined.

The importance of the railroad in opening up the Plains to white migration in a range of ways is a valid point, though the student could have explained more about the impact on the Plains Indians' way of life here.

This paragraph links directly to explaining the importance of the railroads for changing the Plains Indians' way of life and the ways in which it changed.

Verdict

This is a strong answer because:
- it shows a clear understanding of the period
- the student analyses relevant ways in which the railroads were important in changes to the lives of the Plains Indians.

Answers to Recall Quiz questions

Chapter 1

1 Any three reasonable answers, e.g. for food, hide used to make clothes, fur used to make blankets

2 Mexico

3 Problems included: lack of timber to build houses with; lack of timber to build fences with; lack of timber to fix broken tools and implements with; lack of wood to burn for fuel; without trees to act as windbreaks, the prairie winds could flatten crops

4 1851

5 A financial crisis, and it led to a long-lasting economic depression in the USA

6 Bad decisions included: setting off late (May 1846, when April would have given them more time); the decision of the 80 migrants to try the new route; believing that Lansford Hastings had actually completed this short cut; arguing amongst themselves (violently) about which route to take; not turning back when the short cut proved to be much more difficult than expected; deciding to tackle the Sierra Nevada mountains in late October – too late to be safe

7 Three reasons could include: a central plan was developed that worked out the details of what everyone needed to do; the Mormons' religious beliefs meant that everyone followed the plan rather than wasting time arguing over what to do for the best; the Mormons were able to use irrigation in the area from streams feeding into the Great Salt Lake; the Mormons spread their settlements over a wide area and then made each settlement specialise in something that all Mormons would benefit from; the Mormon pioneers were soon joined by large numbers of new Mormon migrants who all helped to build the settlements; Mormons around the world contributed money to the settlements; Mormons believed that God was helping them build settlements in the desert, like the Hebrews in the Bible, which improved their morale and ability to withstand suffering and difficulties

8 False, although it did create the idea of areas of land 'belonging' to each tribe, which was a first step towards reservations

9 The definition in the textbook is: the belief that white Americans had the right to populate all areas of America from East Coast to West Coast

10 To keep Plains Indians and whites apart

Chapter 2

1 The American Civil War ended in 1865 with the North (or Union) victorious

2 160 acres

3 The Union Pacific and the Central Pacific

4 1869

5 Barbed wire

6 Chisholm Trail

7 John Iliff

8 Your answer could include one of the following: filing claims under the Homestead Act for the bits of land on the ranch which contained waterholes or springs; ranch-hands and family members would file Homestead Act claims to parcels of land throughout the ranch area and then hand those rights over to the ranch; by fencing off the ranch's sections in such a way that access was blocked to sections mixed up with ranch lands; by taking homesteaders to court over claims, knowing that most homesteaders did not have the money to pay lawyers and court costs and so would have to give up their claims; by threatening homesteaders with violence, damaging their crops and accusing them of rustling cows from the ranch's herd, which could end up in severe punishments for the homesteader

9 The Bozeman Trail

10 President Ulysses S. Grant

Chapter 3

1 The winter began in 1886 and ended in 1887, so it's usually known as the winter of 1886–87

2 Custer: Lieutenant Colonel George Armstrong Custer

3 The Ghost Dance

4 1883

5 Johnson County

6 The Black Hills

7 The Clantons and the McLaurys

8 Kansas

9 Pat Garrett

10 1890

Index

Acknowledgements

Picture credits
The publisher would like to thank the following for their kind permission to reproduce their photographs:

(Key: b-bottom; c-centre; l-left; r-right; t-top)

akg-images Ltd: IAM 8, 20; **Alamy Images:** Classic Stock 7cl, 44, Everett Collection Historical 29, Glasshouse Images 10r, Granger, NYC 7cr, 32, 50, 62, 65, 73, 84, Interfoto 10c, 56, Joe King 91, Niday Picture Library 88, North Wind Picture Archives 10l, 38, 55, 64, robertharding 87, Wendy White 81, World History Archive 47; **Bridgeman Art Library Ltd:** Private Collection / Peter Newark American Pictures 6, 23; **Getty Images:** Bettmann 43, DEA Picture Library 59, Fotosearch 76, Hulton Archive 24, MPI 12, ullstein bild 94l, 94r; **John W Harman Center/ Duke University Libraries:** 41; **Library of Congress, Prints & Photographs Division:** 33; **Mary Evans Picture Library:** Glasshouse Images 25; **TopFoto:** The Granger Collection 70, 77, 79

Cover images: *Front:* **Bridgeman Art Library Ltd:** Private Collection

All other images © Pearson Education

Every effort has been made to trace the copyright holders and we apologise in advance for any unintentional omissions. We would be pleased to insert the appropriate acknowledgement in any subsequent edition of this publication.

Maps
Map on page 61 used with permission from Claudio Saunt, eHistory.org, the University of Georgia.

Text
Extract on page 14 in Interpretation 1 from Hoebel. The Cheyennes, 2E. © 1978 South-Western, a part of Cengage Learning, Inc. Reproduced by permission.www.cengage.com/permissions; Extract on page 27 in Interpretation 1 "When the trail to Oregon…even in his own land." from The Plains Indians by Francis Haines. Copyright © 1976 Francis Haines. Reprinted by permission of HarperCollins Publishers; Extract in Interpretation 1 on page 53 from *The Great American Desert* New York, Oxford University Press (Hollon, W.E. 1966), by permission of Oxford University Press, USA; Figures on page 51 from Cowboys of the Wild West by Russell Freedman. Copyright © 1985 by Russell Freeman. Reprinted by permission of Clarion Books, an imprint of Houghton Mifflin Harcourt Publishing Company. All rights reserved; Extract on page 90 in Source A from The Frontier Army and the Destruction of the Buffalo, *The Western Historical Quarterly,* Vol.25 no.3, p.331 (1994), The Western historical quarterly by Utah State University; Western History Association. Reproduced with permission of Utah State University in the format Book via Copyright Clearance Center.